Altar Boys, Demons, and More :

Stories, Poems, and Essays

James F. O'Callaghan

Altar Boys, Demons, and More: Stories, Poems, and Essays

©2015 James F. O'Callaghan

Cover photo: James Louis O'Callaghan, b. Kars, Ontario, Canada 1878, d. Seattle, Washington 1970

Tacchino Press
24915 230th Way SE
Maple Valley, WA 98038

PRINTED IN THE UNITED STATES OF AMERICA

Dedication

To Giovanna, John, Neil, Louis, Amy, Laura, Susan, Gianna, Thomas, and all others who have made life so wonderful I wanted to describe it.

Acknowledgements

The following appeared, perhaps in another version, as follows:

"A Rose in May," *Plateau Area Writers Quarterly,* March 2009

"The Fish in the City," *Naples & Beyond: Anthology of the Naples Writers' Circle, 1993*

"How I Tamed a Naples Cat, *Naples & Beyond: Anthology of the Naples Writers' Circle, 1994*

"Memorare in Autumn," *The Latin Mass,* Winter, 1966

"In Defense of Rote Religion," *Homiletic & Pastoral Review,* February 1995

"They're Still Roaming," *Homiletic & Pastoral Review,* June, 2006

"Confessions of a 'Fifties Altar Boy," *The Latin Mass,* November, 1993

"The New Neighborhood, " *Wellspring,* Summer/Fall 1996

"Naples Byways," *Naples & Beyond: Anthology of the Naples Writers' Circle, 1993*

"A New Catechism for an Old Tradition," *Homiletic & Pastoral Review,* January 2009

"Inscrutable in Rome," *Foreign Service Jurnal,* August 1995

"Termination for Cause," *First Things,* November 2004

"Something Sí, Yanqui No", February 23, 2012 in *Curitiba in English* (on-line journal)

"On Finding an Old Latin Book," *PAWA* March 2010

Stories

Poems

O'Callaghan Proverbs 148

Essays

Foreword

The happy child grows up loving his parents and grandparents and knowing all he needs to know about them. Now I wonder about things I can never know.

My father Neil and Grandfathers James and Fred all told jokes and made droll comments. Grandmothers Anna (they shared the name) laughed readily, as did my mother Gladys, and Anna O'Callaghan liked to recite poems in French that none of us understood. (She grew up in Ontario; I don't know if she really spoke French.) My father was a confirmed Democrat of the pre-1970 kind. He died that year and I think I know what he'd have said in the 1980s, but it's speculation, as is my impression that Grandfather James was a Republican.

Except for a few letters in the bottom of desk drawers or stuck in photo albums, and imperfectly remembered conversations, we have no record of their thoughts. I wish I could hear their voices, not the remembered ones they used with children, but the ones they used with themselves when thinking about politics or sports or God, or about their Gladys, their Anna, their Neil and Fred and Jim.

Hence this collection for curious heirs, that I hope will amuse or inform. I include stories, poems, and essays that I still rather like. Things that didn't make the cut rest in file cabinets or old magazines or in the computer.

Most of my articles about the Church pretty much say the same thing *(bring back the old days)*, so I've included only a few. Particularly bad poems are excluded, as are almost all the 200 or so written for an audience of one: Giovanna. She is my inspiration, and the mother and grandmother of those for whom this collection has been compiled.

With love.

A Rose in May

Several years ago I strolled through the narrow cobbled streets of Capri past shops redolent of bread and flowers, and beneath the ever-present death notices pasted on walls, until I found myself by the two cemeteries, one for Catholics and one for foreigners. Sitting on a marble bench, savoring the fresh May air and the sea view, I noticed a bent old man placing a rose on a headstone. The look on his face was so sad, yet so serene, that I could not take my eyes off him.

Perhaps seventy-some years old, he had a dark face such as you might see anywhere in southern Italy. His gray hair retained streaks of black, and he looked well-fed in his faded blue suit. As he crossed himself and walked away, his moist eyes remained fixed on the ground.

There is nothing unusual about placing flowers on a grave, and yet I wondered. Why would a native visit a foreign grave? I walked to the tombstone and read: Elizabeth Percy Pagano, 1922 - 1946.

So: a young woman, probably British, must have married a local man, and the old man must be Signor Pagano. When I returned to Seattle and told my wife about it she wiped away a tear and said "that's sweet."

I sold food-processing equipment in many countries, and it was two years before I returned to Capri. Mary longed to come with me but now her parents needed her; before, it was the children. "One day," she smiled.

This time as I stood at the grave I noticed a woman of perhaps forty years staring at me. I wished her good day and she, nodding toward the grave, asked, "*Lei é parente?*" In my clumsy Italian I answered, "No, not a relative."

"Ah." She sounded relieved.

"And you?," I asked.

"*No, non sono parente.*"

I returned to Capri a few more times more in the coming years. Only once, again in May, was there a rose on it. But another time I saw two elderly women placing a bouquet on Elizabeth's grave and shamelessly eavesdropped, hearing a British accent complain that the flowers cost "three times what you pay in Surrey!"

After arranging the bouquet neatly they stood back and one said "Poor Liz."

Now I greeted them and asked, "Would you be relatives?"

They looked at me suspiciously until the shorter one, in pink, replied, "She was our sister."

"Ah." As she said no more I ventured, "She died very young. It must have been hard for you."

"Yes, it was."

"How did she die?" I asked, hoping they would not think me impertinent.

"She drowned!," snapped the one wearing a gray dress and sweater. Then she grabbed her sister's hand and turned away.

Two years later I was in Capri as a retired man and a widower. Mary would never make the trip now, and I didn't want to. It seemed pointless. But standing by her grave in the Spring I felt that she wanted me to go. The foolish thought remained and became almost a command. "All right," I told her, "But I won't enjoy it." .

Passing through the narrow lanes this time, I tried to imagine Mary's name on one of these death notices -- like the one, faded and barely clinging to the wall, which said *Giuseppe Pagano, Age 83, April 14th.*

I quickened my steps to the Catholic cemetery, passing from one fresh grave to another until I found his tombstone and said a prayer for him and for the wife with whom he was now joined after all these years. And yet, they were separated still. I looked across at the foreigners' cemetery and again saw two women, not the same ones, at Elizabeth's grave. The one in a blue dress was very old; the other, in black, was the woman who had spoken to me years before. With a touch of gray in her black hair she was a younger version of the short round-faced lady beside her.

As I approached they turned away from the grave, leaving one red rose. The younger woman looked at me with recognition dawning in her eyes while the other sighed and muttered *fatto,* "It's done."

"But you're not a relative?" the younger said to me, after the usual polite greetings.

"No. I met her sisters."

"Ah, a friend."

I fell into step beside them as she asked a few questions and learned I was American rather than British, had met the sisters but briefly, and had never met Elizabeth. The next step in Italian etiquette was an exchange of names: Maria Pagano Colonne introduced herself and her mother, Elena Volpe, widow of Pagano.

"My wife was also Maria," I said. "Mary."

"Was?" The old woman looked at me with intelligent, sympathetic eyes.

"Yes, Signora. She died four months ago."

She shook her head. "I'm sorry. I, too, lost my husband. Last month."

We reached a small gate and the mother insisted I come in for coffee, leading me through a courtyard thick with flowers into a kitchen with the lingering odors of *prosciutto* and cheese and pasta. We sat at the table beneath a statue of the Virgin.

"My husband, he renewed this house completely." Mrs. Pagano looked around, inviting me to admire the workmanship. "In 1950 it was a ruin! But Giuseppe said, we'll make it beautiful again!' I didn't believe him! But he did it, and we raised five children in this house. And the roof -- it never leaked!"

I admired the cabinets and the windows and the floor without pretense. As we sipped our coffee I learned how Giuseppe as a child received the best grades in the whole school and, although she lacked details, Elena insisted he had distinguished himself as a sergeant in North Africa before bad luck put him in the hands of the English.

"Or maybe not such bad luck," she smiled softly. "'Giuseppe said it was good luck, because he spent the rest of the war in Wales and not in Russia, and he learned to do carpentry there, in Henllan," she pronounced carefully. "Do you know that place?"

"No, Signora. I've never been there."

"They even built a chapel," she added. Returning home in 1945, Giuseppe found work fixing things neglected during the long war years, using old pieces of hardware to keep his prices down. His unquestioned merits led to a thirty-year career with the *funicular,* the cable-car company.

It was good to hear all this, but I wanted to know about Elizabeth Percy. "I believe I saw Signor Pagano once," I ventured. "Some years ago, in the cemetery." At once I realized I had made a mistake.

The Signora turned away, her face troubled. Maria hastened to fill my small cup explaining that it would be a shame to waste coffee, prices being what they were. I agreed, and described the growing popularity of Italian coffee in the United States until the widow's face relaxed. Then there was nothing to do but thank Signora Pagano for her hospitality and leave.

"I'll go with you," said Maria. "My husband will be home for lunch."

As she closed the gate she said quietly, "You want to know about the English girl."

"Yes. But if it's too painful . . ."

She shook her head. "Not the pain you think. She died before I was born. But she came to our house. Always in May."

We walked silently until reaching the bench by the cemeteries. She directed me to sit beside her and began. "I'll tell you. I'll tell you what I can, because . . . because you truly want to know. And it's a way to remember Papa. And Mamma.

"It's no secret what happened. Everyone knows even if I heard different parts from different people and sometimes they didn't agree. No one in my family ever spoke of it. But we lived with this . . . this ghost. And until today I didn't know how much Mamma loved him. I think you will know how to understand."

I smiled softly, unsure what such a compliment meant.

"This Elizabeth Percy, she came to Capri with the British Army in 1943. Then the British left and the Americans came. But she stayed as a liaison or something for the American colonel, working in an office that distributed food and medicine, anything to help for the people in those terrible years. Old people say she traveled all over the island, and that she was beautiful, and kind, and that she always wore blue to match her eyes. Even when she wore a uniform, she had something blue -- a ribbon or a sweater. She loved the old things, all the ruins at

Casa Jovis, the Greek things, the churches. It seems she had studied these things, their history. And she stayed even when she wasn't in the Army anymore, when the Americans started to leave."

Maria stopped here, took a deep breath and stared into the distance, like a climber studying a crevasse, wondering if he dare cross it. "They say she stayed because of Giuseppe, my father," she said, and fell silent.

To fill the vacuum I asked, "Your father would have returned from England by then?"

"Yes. The two of them met when he asked the Americans for work as a carpenter, or as a translator. He learned English in the prison. Elizabeth needed a translator because although she spoke Italian almost no one understood her. Giacomo Rodi, God rest his soul, he was my father's best friend; he said she spoke 'like a wooden Florentine!' So Papa became the carpenter-linguist of the Americans. Giacomo teased him about it for years, but never in front of Mamma. He told me Papa liked this work, and the family was happy to have the money. But they were not happy for long. And Mamma was never happy."

She took a deep breath, as if preparing to attack the next hill.

"If it wasn't for the war, Mamma and Papa would have married long before. It was what everyone expected, always, and when Papa returned he began to court Mamma again. They would marry when he 'had something set aside.' But after he found work, he stopped coming to Mamma's house every day. He came only five days a week, then three, until it didn't seem like courting at all. He would always say he had to work until one day my uncle -- Mamma's brother -- asked what sort of work he had to do with 'that English ...' and he said a bad word. There was a big argument and Papa stayed away.

"At his house, things went badly. Grandma would ask him how he could abandon his childhood sweetheart, and Grandpa said Giuseppe was disgracing the family by breaking the understanding with the Volpes, Mamma's family, and chasing after a foreign woman who didn't speak our language and didn't know how to cook and wasn't even Catholic. I don't think he really knew she couldn't cook," she smiled, "but he said it. Papa would spread his arms and say 'I can't help it! What can I do? I'm crazy for her! I'm crazy!' My father told Giacomo this, and Giacomo was old when he told me, so probably it wasn't just like that but . . ." She shrugged. "It must have been something like that.

"So Papa spent less time at home. Sometimes he stayed with Giacomo but he made him promise not to talk about Elena. You see, Grandpa had asked Giacomo to 'talk some sense into his head.' He'd even sleep in the woods rather than come home and hear the same old arguments or worse, threats to himself or Elizabeth from my uncles who vowed to protect Mamma's honor."

Maria laughed softly. "It sounds strange now, doesn't it? Who talks of honor anymore, of a woman or a family? But they did, in those days. I don't think any of my uncles would have done anything. They were good, kind men, all of them. God rest their souls. But you never know. Papa was worried.

"But he was happy too. He went to Elizabeth every day, always with a fresh rose that he would present with a bow, and laugh and say he knew that English ladies loved their roses. She said she was glad that Britain had taught her barbarian some manners. Then they would visit every corner of the island. Papa showed her gardens or ruins that most people don't even know about, and she told him things about the Roman emperors who lived here, and the artists who had painted all those good and bad pictures in the churches. They were happy despite his troubles. And hers. She had troubles, too.

"On Capri you always know someone who knows someone who knows something. After the war English people began to come back. Local people who worked for these English families said that while they drank their tea, they gossiped about Elizabeth. First it was just the talk, with lots of laughing. Then the gossip became mean. They said Elizabeth was a disgrace to take up with a carpenter, and a foreigner, and a Catholic."

She stopped here, gazing with soft eyes toward the grave in the non-Catholic cemetery. I made sympathetic noises: "Poor girl. Poor Giuseppe. It must have been very hard, and for your mother, too."

Maria sighed and nodded, and began again. "Everyone agreed this could not go on, this scandal that outraged everybody. Yet it did go on, until Elizabeth's family paid a visit. She introduced them to Papa, and he told Giacomo later that while he was with those stiff English people, who were very cold, not like the ones he had known in Wales, that he -- Papa -- had sat there like a statue and could hardly remember a dozen English words. After he left, Elizabeth and her parents had a big argument. At least, that is what someone who knew someone who worked there said. When her parents left Elizabeth did not go with them to the dock. A week later, she was dead."

I held my breath while she paused, her eyes shut.

"Papa never spoke of what had happened, not even at the inquest. But the magistrate said it was all right, that they could see what had happened. It was enough what Father Cerio said, and his housekeeper, and Giacomo Rodi..

"Father Cerio said yes, he had married Giuseppe Pagano and Elizabeth Percy that night -- May 15, 1946. He knew the family objected but the two persons had their documents in order and insisted it was urgent, that they were leaving Capri within a day. The 'non-Catholic party' -- that's what Father Cerio called her -- promised to raise the children as Catholics, and there were two witnesses, Giacomo and the housekeeper.

"Giacomo loaned his sailboat to Giuseppe, who was going to sail it to Naples and then look for work in Milan or maybe go to England or America or Australia. But, Giacomo said, Papa was sure they could not stay on Capri. And he was afraid to take the ferry because too many people knew them, and someone might do something crazy or at least unpleasant."

She stopped and remained silent while a couple with their two children passed by. Maybe, like me, she was wondering how things might have turned out were it not for those long-ago threats.

"Papa was a good sailor," Maria resumed. "Even when the sky didn't look good, Giacomo thought they would be all right. But then the storm came, so suddenly. It must have caught them as they went by the *Faraglioni* -- you know those huge rocks that rise out of the sea just off the coast?"

I nodded. Yes, I knew the magnificent frightening things that reached up from the ocean floor like the fingers of a god.

"It was on a beach nearby that a fisherman found Papa staring out at the sea, with Elizabeth in his arms.

"Then there was a big fuss. The British Consul said the body must be returned to England. Papa said No. They argued, but then her family sent a telegram saying they didn't want anything to do with it. So they took her to the cemetery for foreigners, and there, every year on that day, on May 15th, Papa put a rose. And three years later he married Mamma."

Maria got up and walked towards the cemetery, staring without seeming to focus. Then she returned and sat down again.

"Your mother must have loved him very much," I said.

Maria smiled. "I know. But I didn't know how much. Well, people said that Papa had returned to his senses, and no one dared tell Mamma that she was a fool to accept him after all that. Mamma and Papa seemed to take up where they had left off, as if there had been no war and no girl from England. Yet she was there, that girl.

"My brothers and sisters and I would feel this tension at the beginning of May. Mamma grew quiet and that made us keep quiet. The worst was on the fifteenth when Papa would put on the blue suit and go out of the house. Only for an hour, enough time to buy a rose and go to the cemetery. He never picked one of Mamma's roses.

"While he was gone Mamma would disappear into their bedroom, or scrub the kitchen floor furiously or scold us for nothing. But never a word about Papa's business. We learned about it from friends who heard their parents talk, but we understood without being told not to mention this at home, not to ask. Now they say you should talk about everything, but why talk when it only causes pain?" She stopped, her dark eyes gazing into the past. In a moment she asked, "Where was I?"

"You said your father would leave for maybe an hour."

"Ah, yes. And when he returned he would walk to the bedroom without a word, right past Mamma who seemed not to see him. He would come out a few minutes later in his everyday clothes and sit down to read the paper, or go work in his shop. A little later he would mention the weather or say there was a new death posted at the corner. After a while Mamma would answer that we needed the rain, or that poor Signora Petri had suffered too much and her death was a mercy. The tension would slowly seep away, like the smell of pasta when you're done cooking. But it never disappears completely. Just enough that you don't think about it. We children would start laughing again. In a day or two, everyone laughed and talked like nothing had happened. It was that way even after we all married. We'd still feel that presence in May and we stayed quiet in Mamma's house, and told our children to play outside."

Maria looked at me. "Do you see? Do you see how she was in our house all these years? Like an invisible guest each Spring?"

"Yes," I said. "I see. It's . . . extraordinary. I don't know what to say. Your father was . . . He loved your mother very much, and yet was faithful to ..."

"He was wonderful. Listen. Three weeks ago we began to remember again, after he died. But this year Papa wouldn't step out of the house and Mamma wouldn't scrub the floor like she was trying to erase the memory of that woman. I thought I was glad we wouldn't have the tension again, but I just felt lost. Can you understand? It was like Spring wasn't coming this year. And if I was going to miss it, miss that unpleasantness, what would the poor English girl think when no one brought a rose? That's nonsense, but it's what I thought.

"I went to mother's house this morning like every day since Papa died, to keep her company. She didn't want to talk about the children or neighbors. Neither one of us said anything about the rose but at ten o'clock Mamma put on her blue dress and said, 'It's time.'

"I stared at her and she said 'Now I must do it for him.'"

"She picked a rose from her garden and we went to the grave, and she put the rose on it. She stared at the tombstone for a long time. Then she said, *'Va bene*, Elizabeth Percy. It's all right.'"

After Maria left I sat for a long time looking at the bay and the mountain, and at the couples strolling hand-in-hand. I thought of other forms of beauty, discovered late and valued the more for that reason, never to be forgotten. I wished Mary could have heard the story, though she always knew it.

The Fish in the City

Michele Caggiano slipped out of Mass early and joined his older cousin Giuseppe walking toward the docks. No danger today of Giuseppe's calling him a pious 'angelino' since he had been in church himself: the death of Gianni Colombo so soon after that other death had driven wives and mothers frantic and the church had been packed with fishermen invoking God and their own San Gennaro; part of Michele was glad the women had insisted: there was something unnatural about the way Gianni had died, as though the sea had forgot the rules. It couldn't hurt to flatter Heaven a little, or to ask that he, Michele, have the honor of killing the unnatural fish.

"O.K., now we have God and San Gennaro on our side," snickered Giuseppe, lighting a cigarette. "Let's all four of us jump in and get the bastard."

The rich familiar smell of fish enveloped them on the docks - - of fresh fish and rotten fish and the ghosts of fish taken and cleaned over the centuries. Along the sidewalk men sold live fish and octupi and crabs and eels from plastic buckets and tubs. The March sun came out briefly and threw bright colors on the previously gray scene, sparking blue on one stretch of the bay, shimmering green over the island of Procida, and translucent white on the ferry boat arriving from Ischia; even the ancient gray half-destroyed buildings above the port received a bath of soft yellows and browns. Both boys breathed deeply and looked about optimistically.

"It will be all right," Michele said, adding in a mock-serious tone, "if the saint hangs around."

"So where's he going to go?" asked Giuseppe.

Where indeed? No place was as beautiful as the Pozzuoli to which they themselves belonged like native plants or fish, their own faces staring back at them from the crumbling Roman murals scattered throughout the city. Both these boys with curly black hair and round eyes and prominent noses might have taken life from one of the innumerable Roman or Greek vases excavated from Paestum or Cuma or Ercolano and now waiting out the current century in museums. Natural and man-made wonders were all around their bay and even in it, like nearby Baia's magical underwater city. They stared in that direction now, as if looking for the spot where Gianni had waited to die, trapped between rocks at the entrance of an underwater cave with his air tanks emptying inexorably. Michele wondered if the damned fish had stayed to gloat.

"Today?" he asked, looking at the sky skeptically as the sun disappeared again, and then at their blue and yellow skiff jerking violently against some sudden bigger waves.

"You can't see anything today," Giuseppe answered, adding smugly, "I'll get it tomorrow."

"You wish." Michele had prayed that if he didn't kill the fish himself, that at least Giuseppe not get it either. "But what if Luigi and that crowd go out today?" he asked. They looked up the line of nearly identical boats. In almost the last one, a man stood talking to two others on the dock. "We'd never hear the end from those braggarts."

They won't go out."

Indeed, Luigi and Giovanni and Pasquale were strolling toward them now, evidently resigned to waiting.

"I can't wait to see their faces when I bring that sucker in," said Michele.

"Fat chance! Just stay out of my way."

Michele glowered but said nothing. What could he say? Giuseppe had never wanted to be his partner and in the two years they'd worked together had found a hundred ways to remind Michele that he fished with him only because his own father had compelled him to help "the little cousin" whom he teased about anything, and most annoyingly about "the precious boat." Michele <u>did</u> care for the boat lovingly, but not because it was his property: his father, killed in the earthquake years before, had shaped and placed and fastened and sealed every plank himself. In polishing or painting those planks Michele felt close to the father whose face he remembered dimly but with great pride: he had died trying to save old Signora Bianchi next door. Giuseppe had never been able or willing to understand this, and even though he now treated his enforced partnership more as a joke than as a real complaint, Michele nonetheless felt patronized and belittled and resented it the more since others followed Giuseppe's lead in teasing him. But not everyone: Gianni Colombo never teased him, and used to talk to him like an equal. This was another reason to avenge him, just as Gianni had sought to avenge the tourist.

They scoffed at the amateurs in expensive equipment who came on weekends to spearfish or explore the submarine city, sometimes getting their gear on wrong or proudly displaying worthless mud sharks. Michele's own snotty comments about the amateurs helped control the fear that settled in his own stomach every time he put on the inhuman aqualung and slid into the foreign world of the sea: surely his professional skill would protect him. He had clung tightly to this comfort two weeks before as he helped cut the Naples engineer from the spear line that had tangled around his neck and legs and the rocks and litter of the underwater city, and load the body carefully into Luigi's skiff. At the sight of the man's blue face Michele wanted to shout "He was a fool! How could he let a stupid fish twist him around like that? Why didn't he cut the line?" But he respected the man's sobbing brother and the dead man himself until later when he and Gianni and all of them comforted each other with this bravado.

They had dismissed the brother's claim that the *sernia* was "huge -- a monster!" Groupers grew large, of course, even to three hundred pounds; but they were slow and stupid as well. No, this was just an amateur accident, as Gianni said, and though the grouper had escaped the first few boats to go after it they all knew they'd kill it soon, just as they killed fish every day.

"*Non si fa niente neanche oggi,*" said Luigi disgustedly as he reached them, his arms spread in eloquent helplessness. Of course nothing could be done today, just as nothing had been done in the four days since Gianni's funeral. *And maybe it will just go away,* Michele hoped guiltily. But he said "No, nothing," and stared at the abandoned buildings on the hill, more decayed than ever since the earthquake: the authorities had closed that most ancient section of the city, forcing Michele and his mother to move to one of the small apartments hurriedly constructed by the government near Pinetemare. He missed his old home but had no desire to return: the memory of that night still haunted him.

"Poor Gianni." Pasquale spoke what was on all their minds.

"A good man," Michele added. "How in hell . . . "

They silently mulled over the question. How indeed could Gianni, a professional with ten years' experience, have let

12

himself be outwitted by a fish? Evidently he had tried to follow the grouper into one of the many caves in the hilly sea bottom and had simply got stuck, like a weekend amateur. Did the damned fish work some sort of charm on him? Even so, that would not explain Gianni's other mistake, his going after the fish alone. you never went alone -- this was the first rule of diving. Had his experience made him so over-confident that even San Gennaro would not or could not protect him?

"He had guts," said Luigi respectfully. And that was also true. So true, and so final, that they could find little more to say and stood around in uncomfortable silence until a squall blew in from the northwest; the rain beat against their backs as they left the docks.

The second floor apartment seemed dark and empty as Michele stepped in, except for the light and the smell of soup from the kitchen.

"Michelino! Where have you been in this rain? What do you want to do, catch pneumonia? Change your clothes!" His mother leaned out the kitchen door, her small frame hardly blocking the light from the window behind.

"Mamma, it's all right," he answered grumpily. He had been looking forward to putting on dry clothes and now she'd taken the fun out of it, transforming it from a sensuous pleasure to a dutiful act of juvenile obedience. He'd rather stay wet.

"What do you mean, 'It's all right'? It's all right to catch cold and die? Well it's not all right to get my kitchen all wet. *Vai!*" As she turned back the weak light from the window strengthened the contrast between the jet-black hair Michele had always known and the advancing gray.

"Mamma, I'm old enough to take care of myself!"

Pierangela Gacciano sighed, laid her large wooden spoon on the kitchen counter and stepped out of the kitchen and across the living room, wiping her hands on her apron. She reached out for his coat but left her hand on his. "I know," she said, a sad smile accenting the wrinkles around her eyes. "But if you take care of yourself, what do I do?"

Shame vanquished resentment. Michele saw an aging woman alone in a small apartment which had never seemed like home, not really: the neighbors were decent enough but they shared none of her domestic memories and told him no stories of his grandfather. Inside, the few pieces of furniture they had salvaged from the old house, and the scratched photographs and plaster saints they had dug from the rubble, could not fill the apartment. And more than emptiness, the place and an absence: his father had never stepped through this door, never laughed or cursed in this living room, or teased his mother in this kitchen. Michele put his other hand on her's.

"*Sta bene, Mamma, sta bene*. I'll change."

Monday was an even worse day than Sunday, storm following squall, so Michele and Giuseppe spent the day in their shed by the docks, mending nets and checking scuba gear and trying to tune their decrepit outboard motor. But as he walked home that night through the now-gentle rain he knew that Tuesday would be bright and clear, the air all the more translucent for the days of rain and they would dive for the fish.

He awoke to look out at the stars and the fading blackness in the east, dressed quickly and had finished his bread and coffee before the sun cleared the hills. His mother had been silently staring into her coffee cup but as he rose to leave she asked, almost angrily,

"I suppose you have to go?"

"Of course, mamma," he answered softly.

She sighed and her shoulders sagged. "You men are so proud of yourselves, so strong and bold and no one can tell you what to do, and you do exactly what . . . something tells you to do."

Michele shifted uneasily from one foot to the other. Then she got up and came to him.

"You have your crucifix and your San Gennaro?" she asked, rubbing his chest softly.

"Of course." Her hand pushed the gold icons across his chest, snagging a hair painfully. "Ouch!"

"Don't do anything stupid," she said. "Stay with the others, with Giuseppe and Luigi and with Giorgio Cuccio."

"Mamma!" he laughed, "Don Giorgio? He's too old and grouchy to be much help."

"He's old because he's smart. Stay with him."

"O.K., mamma."

She kissed him on both cheeks and turned away.

14

Giuseppe was cursing the motor when Michele arrived. "You try the damned thing!" he snarled. Michele let the carburetor drain -- Giuseppe always flooded it -- and soon had them away from the dock and right behind the others, Luigi and the Volpes and Uncle Mario with Giuseppe's two brothers and Mimmo Colombo with Enrique Volpe and Don Giorgio Cuccio with a son and grandson and six other boats. A regular fleet, thought Michele, a war fleet. But in the movies the Americans and British and Germans and Japanese killed each other massively and anonymously far from home. Today the Pozzuoli fleet sought one only and specific fish which had attacked them where they worked and played.

"Damn!" Giuseppe shouted above the noise of the motor. "Luigi has the best place!"

So he did. Ahead of the rest, Luigi and Giovanni and Pasquale were already in front of Baia and stopping right where Gianni had anchored his boat, just meters away from the last anchorage of the engineer. The grouper was probably there, or very close. Michele looked around until he saw Don Giorgio's boat slowing down and drifting toward a point fifty meters farther to sea than Luigi. He steered toward a patch of water this side of Giorgio, hoping none of the others would get there first.

"Where are you going?" shouted Giuseppe. "Go on the other side or we'll be too far out!"

Michele indicated boats heading approximately in the direction Giuseppe wanted to go and shrugged. "It will head for deeper water anyway with all these people!" he shouted laboriously. "We're better off out there!"

Giuseppe frowned and muttered that the kid should learn to navigate.

They dropped anchor just ahead of Mimmo Colombo and Enrique Volpe and soon formed part of a rough circle around the sunken city, with Luigi's boat in the middle.

"I hope Mimmo gets to kill it -- if I don't," said Michele as a shiver went over his shoulders. Partly it was the chill air as he took off his coat.

"_Beh_, you just stay back out of my way." Giuseppe already had his rubber diving jacket on and was swinging his aqualung into place.

Michele wished his own diving gear were better than the old

tank and regulator he had bought used from the Di Giorgios that sometimes cut short his fishing until he got the airflow valve loose, or tightened connections to stop an air leak. It seemed all right now as he swung the thing onto his back and tested the mouthpiece.

"Ready?" Giuseppe sat on the gunwale looking at him through the huge eye of the diving mask.

"Ready." Michele put his own mask in place and swallowed drily, the old fear in his stomach again; had he not felt it, he supposed, it would mean he was not ready to dive.

In the other boats divers were poised, looking at each other as if waiting for a signal. Don Giorgio, who would stay in the boat while his son and grandson plunged in, took command.

"*Ragazzi*!" he shouted. "All together now -- and stay together! nothing . . . by yourself!" Everyone knew that he would have said "Nothing stupid" had he not remembered Gianni's brother was with them. "Let's go!"

Michele heard a few splashes of others falling clumsily into the water until he lay back himself and his own slap-and-splash was replaced by silence; the fear which filled his stomach pushed toward his chest. he rolled over, located Giuseppe to his left and the two of them swam slowly down toward the city. Michele waited for the tightness in his stomach to subside as it usually did once he was busy underwater. Today it took longer.

Thirty feet down the city reflected the morning sun with surprising clarity. The Romans had used a lot of granite and marble here, as well as the soft *tufa*, that still served as the area's basic building material, and even after centuries the harder stones -- those that hadn't been dragged ashore by later builders -- kept their brilliance. But it was the tufa that formed most of the walls which, reduced to two or three feet in height, traced regular geometric patterns over some three or four acres of sloping seafloor. Over there, about where Luigi would be, there was a theater and rich houses and a swimming pool but here beneath Michele the ruins were just as interesting, warehouses or taverns near the old port which had served the summer resort of the Romans and which seemed a living city still, with citizen crabs and pious *spigole* and merchant bass resident in the old rooms and passing each other on the streets. And a warrior *sernia*.

Peering below him Michele saw schools of _farfalle_ flash past, and flat sole wander slowly around the stones, and a good-sized eel. He watched carefully until it slid its dangerous length beneath a wall, into a crack that probably led to one of the many caves here, some natural and some formed by the ruins of the old city and some both, caves that had been incorporated into the storerooms of ancient taverns just as the natural caves throughout the Naples area had served as storerooms or wartime shelters or as smugglers' dens and parking garages.

Beside him Giuseppe moved his facemask in a regular rotation, left to right, then up, right to left; down again, left to right. Well away to either side michele could see the shadows of the Di Giorgios and Mimmo and Enrique. He looked straight ahead in the direction where Luigi and Giovanni and Pasquale must be but could see only a haze of light from above the checkerboard walls. That is where the fish would come from, surely. If it came, if Luigi and the others did not kill it there. Michele checked his spear gun again; the fat rubber sling was stretched in place, taut with enough energy to drive the barbed steel spear well into any fish. _So long as it is just a fish_, he thought darkly. In these familiar waters he understood less than ever how Gianni could have been killed by a common grouper.

After five minutes Giuseppe began to look impatient, and ten minutes later signaled that he wanted to return to the boat and get a net to catch smaller fish or collect crabs. Michele shrugged assent: he didn't like the idea but he could hardly give Giuseppe another reason for teasing him. But Giuseppe didn't get very far: Michele shot after him, grabbed his ankle and pointed violently toward the huge gray mass floating toward them across the ruins.

They had never seen one so big. Rounded and shapeless at best, groupers were always ugly. But this one was so huge that grace or ugliness were irrelevant and it hardly seemed like a fish or any creature at all but rather a massive darkness, a void in creation. Both boys froze as it floated a foot above the old walls directly at them. Michele felt the fear fill his stomach and tried not to move: they had only to stay still and the thing would pass beneath them and continue out to sea. Then they could shoot and miss and explain it later somehow.

Now it was only thirty feet away and perhaps fifteen feet

below them. A spear stuck up from its back, swaying slowly against the water and trailing a line limply behind. So one of the others had shot, unless this was an old spear -- Gianni's perhaps. It didn't bother the *sernia*, which moved as calmly and inevitably as the tide. Yes, this would be a prize to tow into port! But Michele understood now that Gianni and the engineer had died not because they were amateurs or foolhardy but because this was no fish for a man to take with a spear and was not even a fish at all but a monster to be destroyed with explosives or whatever they used for Great White Sharks.

It passed below them and they turned with it. From the back, and moving away, it was still awesome but not quite as terrible. Fascinated, Michele moved very slowly after it, not thinking to fire but just to watch the horrible phenomenon a few seconds longer. Perhaps this movement gave Giuseppe courage, or awoke jealousy: he pushed Michele aside roughly and dove after the fish, aiming his spear.

Goddamn Giuseppe! Who in hell are you pushing? Michele's anger overcame his fear for a moment and he followed, half-wondering if he should raise his own weapon against the fish or against his partner. Then Giuseppe fired. The spear covered the ten feet in an instant and buried itself in the tail, two feet behind the other spear. Giuseppe gestured for Michele to come up and shoot but Michele held back, screaming silently at his partner, *Why in the name of God did you do that? It was leaving! We were safe*! He briefly hoped that the monster didn't notice the insult, or didn't care, or that it would hurry away in panic as fish always did. But no: the beast twisted violently down and to the side and then was coming directly toward them as no fish had ever done. The fear that had prevented his firing now compelled it as the thing loomed huge in front of him and he sent a useless spear into the sloping stupid face where it penetrated mere inches before meeting teeth and bone. Michele had no time for disappointment: before he could move away the monster brushed past him, pushing him aside and then knocking him tumbling through the water with a stroke of its tail

The world was all darkness and pain and worst of all the suffocation with the sudden awful absence of the mouthpiece and most of the air that he'd had in his lungs, all of it smashed away. He kicked furiously unsure at first which way was up until he saw the light through eyes burned by the the salt water that flowed in where his mask had been, and felt something trying painfully to drag him back the other way. His left shoulder was in agony as the straps of the aqualung, somehow wrapped around his left arm, jerked at it with every movement. Fighting dizziness, he reached with his right arm and pulled the straps upward, looking for the mouthpiece and air but found only a broken hose and the smashed regulator. He cursed Giuseppe, slipped the whole thing free, and looked again at the surface miles above him. He sent a prayer beyond it, that his mother would forgive this betrayal and that God would somehow fill the empty apartment. And then the blackness.

Don Giorgio had begun to dive long before he saw any scuba gear and he never tired of telling the younger men how the tanks made them soft, or how he could stay down longer than any of them on one breath. And he warned them not to trust "those things" which could malfunction at any time and when they did not, then "they let you stay down long enough to get in trouble." He had stories enough of men dying in these outfits, or in the older diving suits they had used in the 'fifties and 'sixties, their little skiffs almost sinking under the weight of air compressors and engines. Even his own sons and grandsons laughed at his stubborn conservatism but they were glad to have him in the boat when they dived because no one kept a more distrustful eye on the water, or better interpreted the changing shadows. Perhaps no one else would have understood or even noticed the vague commotion off to his right, and none would have reacted so swiftly.

Michele opened his eyes and shut them quickly again against the bright light. A blow on his back sent a stream of water out of his mouth and set him coughing and he looked again, squinting his eyes open carefully. The sun reflected off the water in the bottom of a boat. Don Giorgio slapped him again on the back and the pain in his chest made Michele come fully awake. He was laid over the gunwale, his head down in the boat, and the old man half-in and half-out of the water shouting in his ear.

"Michele! *Come va? Stai bene?*"

Michele took great gulps of air and looked around at the blue bay and the green hills and the wrinkled angry face of Don Giorgio and felt joy and gratitude beyond anything he'd ever imagined, thankful even for the throbbing in his shoulder. "Yes, I'm all right! Thank you, Don Giorgio, thank you!"

Giorgio gave him one last slap and then pulled himself around the boat to the other side so as to get in without capsizing it. "But what the hell happened down there?" he asked angrily.

"Don Giorgio, it was -- a monster!" Michele panted. "Like nothing you've ever seen. Goddamned Giuseppe shot and it came back at us -- Where's Giuseppe?"

"I don't know, damn it! Was he all right? Could he have gone after the fish?"

"No, he couldn't . . . he shot and it came at us. It was going away and he shot . . . Dio mio, where is he?" Michele turned painfully this way and that looking for Giuseppe to pop to the surface, laughing or cursing.

"You wait here -- I'll go see."

"All right, all right." But Michele knew at once it was not all right to cling to the boat and let an old man find out what had happened to his partner. That is what he would be known for, all his life.

"No, I'll go," he said urgently. "Where's my tank? No, the damn thing's gone! Damn!" He took several deep breathes, exhaling as completely as he could before filling his lungs and pushing off from the boat, ignoring Giorgio's curses, and dove straight down.

Without a mask it was hard to see much but he ignored the pain and studied every shadow, every movement, and looked along the walls of the city and at the stones and to all sides and tried to dive deeper, using his legs and right arms since the left had become useless, until the pain in his chest brutally reminded him that he was reduced to human limits, more out of place than ever in this fluid world. As he turned to go up for air he saw it, or rather he saw what wasn't there, no light, no city, but a moving blankness passing from his left to his right and behind it the squirming figure struggling helplessly against the thin lines that pulled him forward in a hideous parody, a man hauled in by a fish. But Michele could wait no longer.

He burst from the water, drank air as quickly as he could and shouted "Giorgio! It's got Giuseppe! He's tangled in the line! Get help -- get the others -- quickly!" Before he dove again he saw that others were already on their way and, in that small space, would be there in a minute or two. But Giuseppe had only seconds. He reached for his own knife and held it tightly in his right hand and dove, trying not to hear the accusation that might haunt him all his life: *Had you shot earlier, Giuseppe might be alive. Yes*, he would answer pointlessly, *but it's not my fault! Giuseppe himself was to blame and what could I do? Get killed with him?*

Now he could not find the monster. In frustration and guilty relief he alternately cursed and prayed as he swam in the direction it had been moving and was again feeling his lungs complain when the damned thing appeared below him, going in the same direction. He dove straight down and now saw Giuseppe clearly, holding his mouthpiece in place with his right hand while the left was held against his body by the line. Michele cried to him silently *Cut yourself loose!* as his friend was pulled away just beyond his grasp. A shadow shot past him on his right but Michele could not stay to see. On the way to the surface he realized that Giuseppe's knife, in a sheath attached to his left calf, was beyond his reach even if he didn't have to hold the mouthpiece with his right, and even if the turbulence of his passage didn't hold him almost paralyzed. He broke the surface and found his own skiff in front of him.

Don Giorgio surfaced beside him, empty spear gun in hand. As Michele breathed deeply, one hand on the skiff, the old man shouted at him:

"Michele! Wait for the others -- the thing is too big! We need more guns! They're almost here!"

Of course it was the only sensible thing. Michele watched the sun glisten on the smooth gunwale of the skiff and thought confusedly of his father, how nice it would be if together they could admire this good boat; the older man would nod and say that Michele had cared for it well. And he would say that Michele had done all he could for Giuseppe. *Yes, Papa, but you went back to save Signora Bianchi.* He looked about for an answer but saw only the angry face of Don Giorgio and the boat and the sea and Giuseppe nowhere yet terribly *there*, below, dying. He dove again, asking San Gennaro to keep Giuseppe's aqualung working and not to let him, Michele, shame himself before his father and friends.

Again the thing had disappeared. Michele began to swim in its former direction but stopped after a second. Of course. It was circling. He turned around and faced it, coming almost straight at him, five feet below. Something was different: it swam spasmodically, in jerks and twists which caused the four protruding spears to swing wildly. Michele dove down at an angle which took him around the spears in front -- his own, uselessly stuck in the upper jaw and another, surely Don Giorgios's, on the side -- and almost into the violent irregular strokes of the tail. He dodged to avoid the other two spears which looked like ruined masts. He was pushed back a foot by the turbulence but kicked harder, got in behind the fish and closed his legs around the line. He tried to grab the cord with his left hand but the effort produced only agonizing pain in his shoulder and then he was struck from behind as Giuseppe was pulled into him and pushed him forward. He felt the knife loosen in his grasp but reached instinctively and recovered it as his lungs began to complain violently yet again. Giuseppe got an arm around his chest but the feeble grip told Michele there was no time left. *Just save him*, he prayed, just for that and nothing more.

He was sitting on Giuseppe's lap now, both of them dragged by the grouper that seemed to panic, diving and twisting constantly. Michele slashed at the line in front of him but it moved too much and the knife couldn't bite. Twisting his body, he forced his left shoulder and arm forward and ignored the pain as he settled the hand on the line and gripped as tightly as he could. Now the knife bit hard. One, two, three strokes and it broke. Michele kicked toward the distant surface knowing he could not make it before his chest overcame all his own will power and drew in the fatal sea.

The line that he still held tightened and Giuseppe drew up beside him, holding out the broken but serviceable mouthpiece. Michele dropped the knife, blew out the air so painfully held, and pushed the mouthpiece between his teeth. He took three quick breaths and returned it to Giuseppe. Before they reached the surface they saw other divers on all sides and two, Mimmo and Enrique, joined them. Now they had all the air in the world to breathe and when they broke the surface they were laughing.

The return to port took a long time, even with three boats towing the grouper. As different boats came alongside Giuseppe recounted over and over the surprising rare skill of "my man Michele who saved my neck." Michele's heart was too full of relief and remembered fear and gratitude to do or say much more than to punch Giuseppe in the shoulder now and again and mutter, "You almost got us killed, you jerk!" Mainly he looked happily at the most beautiful bay in the world and contemplated all that it held for him, everything he could possibly want. *delle*

They made the final turn toward the dome of *Santa Maria di Grazie* which had served for generations as a landmark. "We'll have to light a candle," he said, and almost without mockery Giuseppe insisted on "a dozen, at least." Michele thought that no matter how it had turned out, someone would light candles. There would always be a reason.

How I Tamed a Naples Cat

There are three things Naples has plenty of: cats, and people, and churches. I spent eight months there and when I left I took two of the three with me. I mean, an orange alley cat with a scar across his nose, and a wife. And I probably wouldn't have got the wife if it weren't for Tiberius. I'd named him that after I read in a guidebook about this really bad emperor because it sounds sort of like tabby which he is except for the color, and because his ancestors might have been housecats to the real Tiberius once. I know that's not likely but when you think about it this cat must have had ancestors going way way back and some of them were almost surely Roman Empire cats. And then he acted like an emperor, like he was just king of the world. Most cats do, I suppose, but Tiberius almost looked the part, sitting there with his chest out and his head back watching you with sleepy eyes like he was trying to decide whether or not to have you thrown off a cliff. Except he was too skinny, especially at the beginning.

Cats just about owned the little narrow street where I rented an apartment from Signora Valente but they were about the most miserable looking bunch I'd ever seen, all half-starved and mangy. They spent most the day digging through the garbage piled on top of these big bins they have there. I might never have had anything to do with them except I bought a used car and Signora Valente said I'd better rent a garage from Luigi Saetta across the way. Naples is a great place for getting your car stolen off the street but they won't usually break into a garage to steal an old Fiat 127. So I did it because the company was paying all my rent anyway. It was part of the deal when they asked me to go teach Italians how to maintain the hydraulic systems on all this equipment they bought from us. I would have paid myself if I had to, just to keep moving. Never was the kind to be tied down.

So Don Luigi gave me the key to this garage that was just part of an old stable they had divided up and I got the padlock off and before I even pushed open the rusty sliding door I heard all this THUMP - THUMP - WHISSH! and when I looked in I saw half-a-dozen cat tails disappearing into the darkness at the back or through a couple little openings six feet up. And one pair of eyes looking at me. Tiberius, he didn't scare that easy. He just sat there on this old wine barrel looking at me as if to say *Just what in the hell do you think you're doing in my garage?* I went in and looked around and he didn't move, not until I got real close and reached out to scratch his ears. Then he hissed once and jumped up into this opening that led off to some other part of the stable. But he didn't run off. No, he sat down there and watched me the whole time I shoved old boxes and scraps of wood and junk out of the way to make room for the car. And when I backed in the Fiat his ears went up another notch but he still sat there, looking not disgusted exactly, but like he might be disgusted if I were worth his while getting disgusted about. But I told him right then, I said I'm paying for this garage and I'm going to park my car here and if you don't like it you can just take your scrawny carcass someplace else. He just glared.

But I've never been one to hold a grudge and I started to feel kind of lonely after a while. They have American TV there from the Navy base so I could watch wrestling and stuff and I traveled all around Italy or as far as I could on weekends but doing that by yourself gets pretty boring and I didn't really have anybody to hang out with. Italians are friendly enough and the guys on this big construction job would invite me out for a drink after work and before I left I'd been in a lot of their houses. I appreciated that because they didn't even need me to teach them about the hydraulic systems which they figured out for themselves real fast. And old Mrs. Saetta, Giovanna, she was real nice too. She and Luigi would be working out in their little garden, them and their daughter Michelina, when I got home and she'd try to chat a little bit and later invite me in for coffee and eventually for a real good dinner which I needed since I can't cook a lick. She pointed at Michelina and said something real fast, meaning Michelina had cooked it. I think. But that not being sure what people said, and not being able to say much, is what makes it lonely in a funny way. It's sort of like you're not really with those people, or not all of you.

I learned some Italian all right but it wasn't ever much more than "staben'" which means OK, and "opan" which means bread, and stuff like that. On the job we worked on "la makina" which is pretty easy because it means machine but it means car too, what I parked in the garage. But once I'd agreed with Luigi that the car was real "bono" even though it was real "evek" which means old, I'd run out of things to say pretty fast. Cats, though, they understand you about as well in English as anything else. Or they don't even pay attention to the words but to the way you say something or how you move. Anyway, I felt like I understood these cats pretty well.

They didn't much care for my taking over their garage but they put up with it and even got something out of it by sleeping on the hood on cold nights. (One time I left the driver's window open and found a bunch of cat hairs on the seat the next morning so I never did that again.) But they stayed real stand-offish, wouldn't let me even get close let alone pet them so I figured I'd train them. It didn't even take that long, they were so hungry.

I just started putting some food out there on the ground, scraps from the table or some dry cat food that one of the bigger little stores sold, and before long, every time I came out and opened the door they'd all show up. Don Luigi and Giovanna and Michelina, they'd laugh when all these "gatti" would come running, but they had to see I was outsmarting those cats. For quite a while they stood off -- the cats, I mean -- until I got out of the way but little by little they'd get closer and closer. Especially Tiberius, he was the bravest of the lot and the only one that got really friendly.

After they got used to coming round I got some real juicy scraps and just sat there with them in the palm of my hand and waited. It was funny the way those cats would look at the meat and take a step forward then look at me and stop and look at the meat again. I don't know what they were so scared of. I never saw anyone doing anything to them but I guess they were just wild. Well, Tiberius he was the first to get his nerve up and he came up real cautious, trying to look at me and the meat at the same time and then real fast he bites into a scrap and runs off out the door. The other cats followed him but I don't think they got any. And before long, there he was again, looking at me and at the meat. He did the whole thing faster this time and the Saettas, who were sitting on this little bench in their garden watching, they laughed and clapped and said "bravo" and Giovanna sent Michelina over to tell me, with a bunch of gestures, that I should come up and have a drink to celebrate. That was nice because we all understood each other and what we were celebrating.

The next day Tiberius came and got the scrap a lot faster and within a few days he was coming right up and getting it and then I'd start to pet him, real slow. And he got used to that, too, like he was getting friendlier as he got fatter. Pretty soon he got to the point where he was purring while he ate out of my hand and he'd come around arching his back wanting me to scratch his ears. The other cats, they never did more than grab something out of my hand and run so I just left some food for them. They probably couldn't help it they were so nervous.

He was just learning to play with a rag on the end of a string when one Sunday night I came back from the mountains and he wasn't there. The other cats showed up, looking a lot more skittish than usual, but not him. I looked up and down the alley to see if there was any orange spot on the pavement when Michelina yelled down from her porch "Ekwi! Ekwi!" and sure enough, there was Tiberius up there eating out of her hand and when I got there he was licking his chops and just purring away like I'd never heard him and Michelina smiling like she was grateful I got him tamed for her.

"What did you feed him?" I asked as best I could and she shrugged and said something. She was scratching behind his ears but Tiberius would twist his head around and lick the palm of her hand every once in a while. I wondered why the other cats weren't all hanging around too but that was just too complicated to ask.

So by Springtime Tiberius had a regular routine. He'd be waiting for me when I came out in the morning and get his breakfast, and when I got home he was having dinner with Michelina and old Giovanna had me join them so much I got into the habit too and time flew and I woke up one morning and realized I only had another month until the contract was finished and I'd have to leave -- either that or stay unemployed in Naples where there's already lots of unemployed people along with other people and cats and churches. So I set about finding out how you import a cat to the U.S. and it's not all that hard once the cat has a certificate about its rabies vaccine and stuff. Trouble was, when I explained this to the Saettas, finally, Michelina looked real sad about it and picked up Tiberius and petted him and looked like she would cry if that cat left and in fact got up and ran into the garden like she didn't want to cry in front of us. Tiberius landed on his feet and looked at me like it was my fault and old Giovanna she motioned at me like I should go try to cheer up Michelina and I didn't think I had much choice.

She was out there on the bench where she used to be every night when I got home and looked so heart-broken that I just about decided I'd leave Tiberius to her and find another cat once I got stateside. I felt real noble as I explained this but she still didn't cheer up and I figured out that she wasn't just fond of the cat and I guess I wasn't either.

Like I said, there are a lot of churches in Naples and I'd visited a lot of them until they all started to look the same, but people mostly stick to their local parish church so we got married in this little one a couple blocks away called something Villanova which may be just a parish church in Naples but had more pictures and statues than most big churches in the States. My new relatives filled it up and even spread out into the street. That's how many there were.

We left Naples just about when I was supposed to but I learned one thing for sure: it's a lot easier to get a cat into the U.S. than it is a wife. But we got here and Tiberius settled in real well and now he acts like he owns my garage and the yard and you don't see any stray cats or dogs either come wandering in. He must just look mean because he's too fat to chase them or fight much. Not that I can say much about that anymore, eating "pasta" all the time. Michelina won't let him in the house because she has this thing about cats smothering the baby or something, but he doesn't mind. He just sits out there in the sun with me, thinking about his next meal I guess. And Michelina seems pretty cheerful despite the language problem but I know how tiresome that is and figure that's why she's still not really herself yet. She hardly ever pets Tiberius anymore.

February 1994

The 1937 Philco

James F. O'Callaghan

Richard found it while looking for the ping-pong ball that his brother, even further into middle age than himself, had slammed into the unfinished part of the basement crowded with lawnmowers and the washing machine and tools and old newspapers. He could just make it out in the light from the doorway.

"That's Papa's old radio!" he shouted.

"What? Can't you find it?" Mike asked.

"No -- I mean, that's the radio!"

"What are you talking about?" Mike appeared at the door, paddle in hand.

"That's Papa's old radio there."

Mike looked at the dusty Philco beside a broken bicycle. A bundle of newspapers was on top of it and, on top of them, a box that said "Super Auto-Vac."

"I know," he said. "So can't you find the ball? Eyes going bad?"

"Not yet."

Mike flipped a switch and half-a-dozen fluorescent tubes lit up the clutter. "Over there," he said. "Beside the table saw."

Richard picked up the ball and then gently ran his hand across the dark wood of the waist-high radio. "Still work?" he asked, idly turning the brown Bakelite knob which adjusted volume and bass and turning. There were also buttons for pre-set stations, some of which, like KTB, no longer existed .

"Did last time I tried it, ten years ago or whenever. Come on, you afraid to lose or what?"

Richard slipped his finger off the last knob, that one to select short wave bands, and stepped away from the radio reluctantly. "Isn't it going to get ruined down here?"

"Hasn't yet. I guess. Come on." Mike turned out the lights.

Mike's last point had brought him to within two at 19-17, but Richard took the next two points the way he usually took them, patiently returning everything until Mike made a mistake.

"That's two out of three," Richard announced, breathing hard. He took off his glasses and wiped his forehead. "Had enough?"

"Hell no." Mike took off his checkered shirt and threw it on top of the sweater he had earlier dropped on the chair in the corner of the crowded room. Sweat darkened his T-shirt, making his pot belly more prominent. "Best three out of five." he added grimly.

"And then it'll best out of seven," Richard sighed in mock fatigue, "just like old times. Better get your breath first, big brother. You're not as young as you used to be."

"I'm not the one getting ready to retire." Nonetheless, Mike grabbed his can of beer from the windowsill and sat down on another folding chair crowded against the knotty-pine wall.

"God, I haven't seen that thing for years," Richard said. "You remember listening to 'Sergeant Preston' and 'The FBI' on it?"

"Sure, and 'The Green Hornet' and 'The Shadow.'"

"'*The Shadow knows*,'" Richard intoned in a dark voice.

"It was better than TV.".

"So how come you don't use it?"

Mike shrugged. "Kids had their own damn stereo making noise, and it didn't get FM and they don't have 'The Shadow' anymore. Come on -- my serve."

Richard got into position, paddle at the ready. Mike hit the first serve into the net.

"Thanks. Zip - one. I would have thought you'd . . . want to, you know, keep it . . . around where you could see it." Richard's words were interrupted by lunges right and left as Mike tried to set up a winner, which he did after three exchanges, angling the ball sharply to the right after moving Richard left.

"Good shot."

"Oh I still have 'em," Mike said smoothly. "Just that I get rusty with you running off to New York and Europe to avoid me."

"Afraid to play with your grandkids?" Richard took the next point.

"They don't hang around long enough, when they come. Tried to play with little Tony but he just hit the table with the paddle -- needs to grow another foot or so."

"So did you win, Grandpa?"

"Twenty-one – fifteen."

Richard retook the lead at eleven - ten. "So you plan to do anything with the radio?"

"I dunno." Mike served again. "Maybe one of these days. Why? You want it?"

"We'd have plenty of room. The furniture we brought back won't half fill up that place."

"I dunno," Mike frowned. "Hey, remember the time I tried to take it apart? I thought Papa was going to kill me!"

"Oh Christ! First of all he was afraid you were going to get electrocuted because you left it plugged in. Then he found out it didn't work anymore. He was not a happy man."

Splat! Mike slapped a drive off the corner to tie the game. "He cared more about that damn radio than he did any of us."

"Well . . . "

"No kidding, he did. More than me, anyway. Wouldn't even let me put it back together."

"Could you have done it?"

"Sure -- the speaker was disconnected is all. But he takes it to the damn shop and then for years afterwards I hear how I cost him fifteen bucks."

Richard had won the last three points as Mike tried too hard to hit winners. "But he was joking," Richard said, "at least after a while. It became a joke with him."

"Wasn't any joke. And every time he had a gripe, when I dropped out of school or wrecked my car or got laid off here he'd come again -- 'Just like when you screwed up the radio and cost me fifteen bucks!'" He hit another ball far off the table.

"Well, he was that way. He didn't mean anything by it."

"Not with you maybe, the altar boy and paperboy with good grades who never screwed up."

"Hey, can I help it if I'm perfect?" Richard smiled in mock humility as he hit the ball into the net. "Damn! There goes perfection."

"Fifteen - twelve. I got you now."

Richard served low to Mike's backhand. Mike returned a weak shot and Richard tried a slam of his own which missed.

"Hmm. Fifteen - thirteen. But your stock went way up when you got married before I did."

Yeah," Mike answered sarcastically. "And he asked me how I was going to support a family with my lousy job."

"That was his way of asking if you needed any help. Anyway, don't you remember how happy he was when Joe was born? Sixteen-thirteen," he added as Mike netted a ball.

"Yeah. It even made him think Rosy might almost be good enough for the family."

"Come on. He liked Rosy."

"You think so? He sure didn't think she was in Laura's class, college girl and all that." Playing more carefully, Mike won two points in a row.

"Fifteen - sixteen. That's funny. Laura always thought Papa liked Rosy better -- he talked to her more."

"He did? Not that I saw." Another slam went wild.

"Fifteen - seventeen. Sure. Laura even thought they were pretty close, closer than she was to Papa. Only natural, since we were gone most of the time and you guys saw them every week."

"To hear him talk about you -- 'My son the bank vice president in London' or wherever."

"Did he do that?"

"All the damn time. Ha! Sixteen - seventeen!"

"People always talk about whoever's not there." Richard kept his voice casual.

"Sure."

"Well, 'God mend him all road ever he offended.'"

"That poetry or something?" Mike asked in sort of a sneer.

"About the only line I remember, about a blacksmith who died. By some priest."

They played the next five points in silence, tying the score at twenty-all.

"Got to win by two," said Mike needlessly. "My serve." He won the point and flipped the ball to his brother. "Your serve. So, you really want the radio?"

32

"Yes and no." He undercut the serve deeply and it died before Mike could reach it.

"What the hell does that mean?" Mike served a low fast one which Richard missed. "Deuce!"

"I'd rather have it in my living room than going to waste in your basement. But on the other hand, Papa wanted you to have it."

"He did?" Mike stood back from the table.

"Sure. That's what he said." Richard stood with the ball in his hand and looked at his brother.

"When did he say that?"

"The last time I saw him -- before we moved to Chicago. We both knew he didn't have much longer and sort of talked around it -- you know how it was -- and somehow the radio came up and he said he wanted you to have it. Didn't he tell you? The way he said it, I thought it had been all decided."

"Damned if I remember that." Mike stared at the table in deep thought. "Maybe he said something . . . take care of it maybe?"

"Well . . . ?"

"I don't know. I must have thought he wanted you to get it in good shape or something. I was surprised when you didn't take it."

"I would have loved to take it."

"Oh."

"Well, you ready?" Richard raised the ball to serve.

"Ready."

They both played carefully, Mike almost visibly constraining himself from swinging too hard, Richard as careful to keep the ball landing low and deep but safely away from the edges. He was too careful: Mike slammed back two softly-looped balls for the winning points. "Two - all!" he smiled.

"No big deal. I'll just win in five, or seven or nine like always. But I do need another beer first."

"Come on." Mike led the way to the unfinished part of the basement, turned on the lights, and took two beers out of the refrigerator near the workbench.

"You're the only guy I know keeps a refrigerator just for beer."

"Hey, saves me climbing the stairs. That can be bad for your heart."

They pulled the tabs and drank, and looked at the radio. "Let's see if it works," Mike said. He took the newspapers and the box off the radio and carefully turned it around to find the plug.

"Damn. Need an extension." He rummaged in a shelf under the workbench, pulled out a heavy yellow cord, plugged it into a wall outlet, strung it across the floor and connected the radio.

Richard pushed a button and both of them watched in wide-eyed expectation as a yellow glow lit up the dial. After ten seconds static and a low hum came from the large speaker hidden behind six lengths of hardwood; Mike carefully turned the tuning dial until rock music blared out.

"It ain't 'The Green Hornet'" he said, turning down the volume.

"No, but it sounds pretty good. The sound, I mean, not the music."

They tried other stations and were amazed that the old tuner could still pull in signals from a hundred miles away, even down here in the basement. Mike ran a piece of wire to the window as an antenna and they tried the short wave bands, and smiled in surprise and satisfaction as the chirping of Morse code or the clipped accents of the BBC came out not quite cleanly but as it were with rust, passing through a speaker too long silent. Mike got a rag and dusted the radio's many strange angles and crevices while Richard sought out the voices that spoke to them again out of the night sky, arriving with the light from stars perhaps long dead, perhaps not.

Flying

Leonard sat on the rock wall in front of Mrs. Gibbons' house and watched the game of kickball, staring morosely at his younger sister Laura. She'd even taken his baseball hat, saying that she needed it now and he didn't. His dull sandy hair stuck out from the top and both sides of his head. When the action moved into the Friday afternoon sun he shaded his dull brown eyes with a dirty hand.

He didn't understand why Mike had called for Laura to replace him. Hadn't he chased down the ball when Tommy kicked it along the sidewalk they called "right field"? And hadn't he thrown it to first base like they always told him to do? But Mike just shouted "The play's at second, dummy!" Leonard wished it was tomorrow already. They couldn't make him sit out on his birthday.

Maybe it didn't matter. Maybe he'd still get his turn to kick the ball and run to first base. Usually they told him he was out. Try as he might he couldn't kick the ball very far with his short legs, and even less could he kick it where he wanted to, up the cul-de-sac which was "left field." Sometimes he'd just trip over the ball and even when he got it to left field things didn't always work out. If he went from first to second the ball would get there first and they'd tell him he was out. If he stayed at first they might yell at him to keep running. The game was complicated and got all mixed up in his head, like the arithmetic problems at school. Even in the special class he was in now, the teacher talked too fast until *two* and *five* and *plus* got all mixed up with the *B* for *Boy* and *minus* and *take away* and *V* for *Vase*.

Before he could kick again, or be passed over, his mother came out on the porch and shouted down the cul-de-sac that it was time for dinner. Leonard was content to go.

As he walked up the slight hill Leonard noticed his father Tony in the driveway looking at him with that look he got on his face sometimes, like the time he came home with a dent in the car.

"How's it going, kiddo?" Tony asked, rubbing his son's head as Leonard mounted the steps.

35

"All right," Leonard shrugged.

"Big day tomorrow!" Tony said enthusiastically, wondering if he'd heard frustration or anger or anything at all in the boy's tone.

"It's my birthday," Leonard said flatly. His father sighed and put an arm around him as they went in the house.

The next day proved as big as anything Leonard imagined. For months he had watched George, from three blocks away, buzz past on his power scooter but hardly dared dream his parents would ever get him one. They must cost a lot of money, and every time he mentioned that a scooter would be "a neat thing to have," his mother would shake her head and say, "A great thing to kill yourself with!" So after breakfast when his father smiled and said he needed help in the garage, Leonard reacted as if faced with a chore. Nonetheless, he began to hope as the family passed through the laundry room to the garage.

It was red, with two small thick tires on either end of the platform, and a small black engine by the rear wheel and handlebars with thick rubber grips. Even standing still, slightly elevated by the two-pronged kickstand and with a big red bow around it, the machine seemed to glide through the shadows. The boy touched it cautiously.

"Think you can handle that?" his father smiled from the doorway, hope written on his face.

"Yeah," Leonard muttered seriously, looking at the scooter.

His parents sighed together. "Never laughs," she whispered sadly.

"Well, he never cries either."

"I get to ride it too!" proclaimed Laura.

Leonard looked at her with no expression on his face.

"You have to be careful," his mother warned.

"And for that," Tony said, here's something you'd better open. He reached up to a shelf and grabbed a box with birthday wrappings and handed it to Leonard who began scraping at the wrapping. The box fell to the floor where Leonard knelt and continued tearing until a box with a picture of a helmet appeared. He struggled to open it until his father squatted down and pulled out the cardboard tabs that held the lid in place.

"You've got to wear that, every time," Tony warned somberly as the boy lifted the black plastic helmet from the box and tried to put it on his head. "This is the front, here," his father advised, turning it.

"Can I ride it now?" The unusual enthusiasm in the boy's voice made his father smile.

"Not yet, sport. You've got to know what you're doing first. Now pay attention." He spent the next fifteen minutes carefully explaining how to fill the gas tank from the same plastic gas they used for the lawn mower. "Be sure the spout is on tight -- and close the can tight when you're done!"

"I know," Leonard muttered impatiently.

Tony pointed out the pedal for the rear brake and the lever for the front one. "Always use the pedal first!" He showed him how to start it with the choke and the pull cord, and let him rev the engine with the throttle; he demonstrated how to put the scooter in gear.

Leonard starfed blankly at the demonstrations. But after he had himself identified the brakes and started the engine and stopped it, Tony looked satisfied. "Now I'll show you first, then you take it."

His father stepped on the scooter and rode slowly down the driveway, Leonard beside him. "Just get your second foot up after you're going. It's real easy to keep your balance," Tony advised. "Easier than a bike, because it's lower, and you just lean a little bit to steer. Just a little bit -- it doesn't take much."

Leonard looked resentful as he jogged alongside. When they got down to the feeder road Tony stopped. "O.K., now look: you can see a good block each way. Always look both ways before you start out! And when you come to the curve, stop! Take a look before you start again, O.K.?"

"Yeah."

"And if you see a car coming, just pull up on the sidewalk and stop, OK?"

"OK."

"Got your helmet on tight?" Tony pushed the smooth plastic back and forth to be sure it was snug. "O.K., champ, take it away!"

The boy put one foot on the platform and slowly turned the throttle. He took a couple steps before bringing up his second foot. The scooter wobbled a little bit but as he increased speed it soon stabilized.

The *zzzz-bam-bam-bam* of the engine increased as he turned the throttle. Then he cut it back and the sound diminished. He turned the throttle jerkily until it was fully open and the engine pitch increased to a satisfying roar as he approached the curve.

"PEDAL FIRST!" his father shouted.

Leonard stepped on the brake pedal but the scooter still wanted to push forward.

'BACK OFF THE THROTTLE!"

Leonard did so, and came to a sudden stop. He wheeled the scooter around to start the other way as his father caught up.

"Look both ways before you go," Tony panted.

Leonard did so. Then accelerated, wobbled, and settled down again as he drove past the cul-de-sac and up the incline which ended in a curve. The scooter slowed as it climbed and at the top was moving slowly when he stepped on the pedal and then gripped the hand brake. The engine died. He stepped off and stared at the scooter.

"Let off the throttle before you put on the brake!" Tony reminded him when he caught up, breathing heavily.

"I forgot. Should I start it again?"

"Yeah."

Leonard jerked on the rope and the motor came to life. He jumped on but before he could leave his father pleaded, "Look both ways first!"

Tony was tired but satisfied after another fifteen minutes of running back and forth behind the scooter. Leonard remembered to cut the throttle. He remembered to look both ways and he went to the sidewalk when a car appeared. His father finally went back to the house and kept an eye on him from the porch. Leonard wasn't aware of him.

The wind against his face and chest seemed like a battle he won constantly. Push as it might against his nose and eyes and the sandy hair that stuck out beneath the helmet and even into his mouth as he laughed, the wind could not stop his triumphant progress up and down the street, to the top of the hill and back again. He stopped only when he chose to do so, his right hand commanding the motor to near-silence, his right foot initiating the drag just behind him as he stepped on the pedal, and his left hand bringing the scooter to an ever-smoother stop as he learned to engage the front brake slowly. Mike and Tommy and all the neighbors seemed to stare in admiration as the roaring engine caught their attention. The noise was like a magic thing, creating the wind through which Leonard pushed unfailingly.

He reluctantly gave up the scooter to Laura when, after standing on the sidewalk and screaming at him for ten minutes, she finally brought her father down. Leonard stood glumly as she went back and forth, starting and stopping smoothly. "My turn now!" he said each time she passed.

He got it back for only a few moments when his father asked if he didn't want to let the other kids have a chance. "You tell them how to do it"

Leonard reluctantly gave instructions to which Mike and the others barely attended before buzzing off. Tommy was on it when the engine died.

"What'd you do?" Leonard asked angrily.

"I think it's out of gas."

They filled the tank and, after a couple pulls, the engine was running again. Though it seemed to Leonard that the other kids rode forever, most made only a few passes before handing it back with a smile. "That's really cool," Mike said appreciatively.

Leonard rode until lunchtime, stopping only to refill the tank. After lunch he ran to the garage and put on his helmet and started it again. Through the afternoon he rode back and forth, back and forth, savoring the wind in his face, and his increasing ability gently to guide the scooter close to the curb or between two oil spots, to make it accelerate or slow or stop or turn in ever-smaller circles. George came by on his own scooter and admired the new machine, and they had a race up to the last driveway before the hill. Leonard won and smiled to himself, oblivious to his father on the porch, to the smile mirroring his own. And he was oblivious to the irritated stares of the neighbors as they followed the roaring buzz up and down the street.

The next day Leonard reluctantly put the scooter in the garage when it was time to go to church, where thoughts of the wind in his face left him no room for prayer. Afterwards he rushed through lunch and resumed his steady roar up and down the street, using the sidewalk to avoid the pickup games of kickball or basketball. Again neighbor kids asked for a turn but soon returned the scooter and he again went up the street and down, past the trees that lined the spring-green lawns, past the homes of his friends, and past the men who stood in driveways talking to each other and staring at him. He gave it up twice to Laura in response to her pleas, and quit for the day only when it began to rain and his mother insisted.

Every day after school Leonard rode, losing all memory of math class and reading class and comments on the bus or in the playground. They were all swept away by the noise and the motion and the control. He even took a sort of pleasure in watching it from a distance, when he turned it over to Laura or a neighbor kid. Sometimes, yielding to his mother's pleas, he would park it and join a kickball or basketball game but soon dropped out to resume his passage along the street where he would have worn ruts by now, had the scooter weighed much more than it did.

On Wednesday, late in the day, as he passed the gray house two doors up Mr. Murphy stepped out of his driveway and put up a hand. "How long do you plan on riding that thing?" the old man asked, a scowl on his deeply-lined face.

"'Till dinnertime, I guess," Leonard answered, looking at the man with puzzled eyes.

"Wish you'd give it a rest," Murphy muttered, turning back to his house.

Leonard wondered what that was about as he started off again, leaving Mr. Murphy and his scowl in the ever-present, ever-receding roar of the engine.

When his father got home Leonard pointed the scooter toward the garage. Mr. Murphy, close behind him, greeted Tony and began talking about weeds. Leonard immediately got bored but sensed something else was going on here. He went into the garage and stopped at the laundry room to concentrate on the low detached phrases from the driveway. He heard "driving me nuts" and "licensed to be on the street?"

Toward the end of dinner Tony said casually. "Looks like you'd better hold down the riding, Sport. Just an hour after school, and a couple hours Saturday morning and afternoon."

"Why?" Leonard let his fork fall on the plate.

"Well, it's sort of loud, you know, and we have to get along with the neighbors."

"Why should they care?"

"Well, they do. But hey, you can still ride it everyday and, anyway, don't you want to get back to kickball and basketball and all that with the guys?"

Leonard turned away. Had he not done so, his father would have seen the first tear to run down the boy's face in years.

Inscrutable in Rome

She was a first-tour Econ officer and he a junior consul, and Brian loved Diana but she spurned each fond advance. Wisdom urged him leave this hopeless quest, yet when has love been wise? His heart was hers from the moment she exulted, majestic and beautiful in the Sexual Harassment Workshop, "Any man tries that with me, I don't care if it's the Ambassador, I'll punch him in the mouth!"

"Noble Diana!" he named her, and *Bold! Alive!* And *Vibrant!* But she was also Cold and Distant, and changed his name to Grief: if love denied is torment, love despised in Rome is Hell. Venus mocked him from her thousand statues, and Eros jeered wherever Brian walked. He might have died for love, wan and wasted on the Spanish Steps or drowned in the Trevi Fountain where he cast his hopeful coins, but first the gods took pity in their playful Roman way.

Suspicious Diana frowned on learning, at the second Pre-Pre-Advance Countdown, that she would be the Inscrutable Control Officer. She turned plainly angry when the White House Pre-Pre-Advance Officer confirmed that Yes, he referred to that Inscrutable, the President's cat.

"You wouldn't assign a man to babysit a cat!"

"Ms. Ventura," interrupted the DCM. "I myself walked LBJ's beagles in Cairo."

Diana flashed angry eyes at the bespectacled pot-bellied man at the conference table, and mumbled that State probably had no women then.

"This is important," droned Pre-Pre-Advanceperson. "The President is very fond of her cat, a gift from the King of Siam, as is Mr. White. I mean, Mr. White is also fond of the cat. It is important the First Family feel at home as much as possible so they can concentrate on their official duties. Now then, Bob, if you'll continue with the assignments?"

Surely she needs sympathy now, Brian thought, and (again) *Faint heart ne'er won fair lady*. He overtook her in the hall.

"Diana!" he cried through the heavy murmur of bureaucrats. "Tough break. I mean, I wish . . . you know."

"Easy for you to say. You get -- what'd you get?" She had stopped, and Brian's heart leapt: she had never asked a personal question before, nor stood this close. He had not realized how blue her eyes were, nor noticed the yellow highlights in her red-blonde hair, nor seen her complexion change from alabaster at the forehead to soft rose petal on the cheeks.

"I said, 'What'd you get?'"

"Me? Luggage. I got luggage."

"Oh." She started down the hall again.

"It might not be so bad," he offered. "You might get to meet the President!"

"Sure, as Kitty Litter Control Officer." She walked faster. He tried to keep up but the slow fat bureaucrats made it impossible. He reached the elevator as she squeezed into the last space.

"They say it's a really nice cat," he said feebly, as the door shut.

The huge airplane crawled loudly across the tarmac, drowning out the sound of applause. Dignitaries scurried to look dignified, and Security to secure, and Brian jumped into the truck to join the fleet of vehicles swarming around the plane. As in the practice drills, they reached the cargo door in precisely one minute and twelve seconds, just as the crew secured the conveyer belt.

Each piece of luggage would have the owner's name and hotel assignment, and Brian had to see that they were loaded in the right sequence: Hotel Excelsior last on, because first off. He reminded the crew to double-check everything, for even though the luggage of the really important people was going by other means to Villa Taverna, the Ambassador's-residence-made temporary-White House, a misplaced suitcase here could send a Sub-Secretary to the Quirinale in a rumpled suit. Embassy janitors and drivers and clerks, pressed into service for the Visit, concentrated grimly as Brian dealt with incomplete or missing tags; consulting his room list he deduced the missing information and directed firmly, "Excelsior!" or "Ambassador!" or "Europa!" In precisely twenty-two minutes they were racing for Rome behind the flashing lights of the Carabinieri. And she was ahead in the darkness: the White House luggage, including the cat, had left almost at once. But he would catch up with her somewhere, somehow, and sometime she would be kind.

He was boarding the shuttle for home when his cellular telephone beeped.

"Brown! Where's Simpson's luggage?"

"Simpson?" Brian repeated.

"Right. Gloria Simpson, White House Chief of Staff. Don't tell me you never HEARD OF HER!"

"Sure, George, . . . Sure, the Europa. That one didn't have the right tag, just a sort of leather thing -- but I found him on the list. Only it's Howard Simpson."

"That must be some communicator or something! THIS Simpson is at Villa Taverna! TA-VER-NA! Capeesh? That's the President's Chief of Staff! She stays with the President! You get that suitcase to the Residence right now!"

"YOU DON'T HAVE TO SHOUT!" Brian shouted. "I'll handle it. But all the Taverna stuff was supposed to be separate."

"Yeah, I know, I know. But someone screwed up and I've got the Ambassador on my back."

"O.K., George. No problem."

As he walked quickly to the motor pool Brian consoled himself that he might see her at the Residence, both of them insignificant among the VIPs. They'd trade airport stories and laugh together. He mused on possibilities even as a red-eyed Howard Simpson denounced the injustice of being awakened by some idiot who couldn't read tags.

Where presidents sleep, no underling may drive; thus Brian afoot endured the Secret Service, their ID checks and suitcase search and consultation with "Control." He gladly left behind their stony faces -- implacable as angels barring Eden -- to walk the long and lovely tree-lined driveway to the Villa.

City noises faded and died, returning the perfumed night to primordial peace and promise .

And suddenly she was there, her still form white marble by moonlight, as if some jealous god had turned her to stone rather than lose her to Time! But then she moved gracefully toward a bush and bent down, and he heard her say, "Here, Kitty, Kitty!"

"Diana . . . he called softly.

She turned. "Brian! How you doing?"

He thought he would die.

"Fine, fine. And you look . . . " He must not offend. "You look for the cat. Yes?"

"Yeah. The First Gentleman was real specific: 'Inscrutable needs his walk. Inscrutable doesn't like a leash!'" She mimicked the famous voice. "And now Inscrutable has hid somewhere. Great."

"Diana . . ."

"What?"

"Oh, nothing. I just wanted to say, I really like that name."

"Inscrutable? Good name for a Siamese, I guess. Except it's racist. Ah, there he is."

The biggest cat Brian had ever seen strode across the patch of grass, its tail high in the air and its sharply-pointed ears testing the four directions.

"Big sucker, isn't he?" asked Diana.

Brian nodded, afraid to speak and not to speak lest he break this magic moment in which fair Diana spoke him fair. "Big," he croaked.

"Bet he'd eat these Roman cats alive."

Perhaps in that moonlit circle words had power to summon, for at that moment a Roman cat appeared from some park or street or ruin. It looked miserably insignificant creeping beneath the manicured bushes, dashing ahead a few feet and then crouching fearfully. But Inscrutable found it significant.

"Uh-oh," said Diana. "What kind of cat is that?"

"Just a regular Roman cat, I guess . . . oh. Ah. I see."

Inscrutable on stiff legs stalked the scrawny feline which began to utter a baby-like wail.

"Oh hell," muttered Diana. "We gotta grab him. You cut him off and I'll sneak up behind him."

"Right."

Brian moved carefully to place himself between the Siamese and the Roman cat. The latter stayed frozen while the former looked up at him indignantly. Diana crept on silent goddess feet toward Inscrutable, who now changed course to maneuver around Brian, who moved right as the cat moved left, like they were playing one-on-one.

Inscrutable stopped. Brian stopped. Inscrutable right, Brian left. Diana was almost on him. He moved to his left and forward; Brian moved right and backward, and stepped on something soft. A high-pitched eerrooRAWOW! pierced his skull as claws raked his ankle. He yelled and jumped and Inscrutable jumped and Diana jumped and something scurried away and then Brian was on his back with Diana's elbow on his chest; she held desperately to the Siamese's' tail and the cat, looking to escape, scratched its way twice across Brian's face. Then it turned on Diana, biting her thumb deeply. She screamed and the cat vanished into the darkness.

Diana held her wounded right thumb in her left hand and wailed sort of like the cat. "Goddamn horny bastard!"

"What'd I do?"

"Come on, we've got to find them!"

Instead of cats they found Secret Service agents, who told their lapels to "be advised two Embassy personnel report Saratoga missing." Which brought dozens of people from the Residence. A very tall woman, who identified herself as Gloria Simpson, took a radio from one of the agents and began barking orders. The ground lights came on and, organized by a dozen conflicting voices, diplomats and drivers and cooks and agents spread out to search the exquisite spacious gardens.

Brian and Diana avoided the hostile sleepy eyes all around them but no one said anything except Simpson, who demanded "Where's my suitcase?" before she disappeared. No one else dared disappear and they wandered through the night from bush to cranny to shed until the dawn brought two busloads of sailors and Marines from Naples; soon after, Brian and Diana were sent away.

The DCM assigned both of them as search party liaisons "for the duration," and although not in her party, Brian was happy to be out looking for the cat. Finding it would win gratitude, perhaps admiration. Perhaps more. In any case, it was better to search for cats than to placate White House aides or edit transcripts. He even enjoyed his widening tour of Rome -- by the second afternoon they had searched from the far end of the Borghese Gardens to the Piazza del Popolo -- except for the grinning Marines showing him scrawny cats and asking, "SIR! IS THIS THE FELINE SIR?" He'd growl back, "Stow that crap, Marine!, but couldn't stop their speculating about "that blonde number who screwed up bigtime." They had no right at all to imagine the gratitude of moon-bright Diana.

He saw her next in twilight, in the Embassy parking lot where the President would greet the staff -- an event to which even the disgraced were summoned. But his joy at seeing her was chastened by her tired troubled eyes.

"Maybe I can get a job on one of those tourist buses, pointing out the Vatican to senior citizens from Des Moines," she said bitterly.

"You'll never have to do that, Diana." *Promise*.

"All my life I'll be Diana Ventura, The Woman Who Lost the Cat."

You don't have to be Diana Ventura all your life.

"You know what Bob told me? 'Find the cat or get on the plane.' Like I'm not miserable enough already, he has to stomp on my face."

"Well, he's the DCM, Diana. It's his job."

The assembled staffers stirred when a parade of important paper-carriers emerged from the Consular Section door. Then the Ambassador appeared to announce "the President of the United States!" and suddenly she was there in the floodlights, the President herself, and the First Gentleman! The staff applauded and cheered the familiar faces so long known to all of them.

"Hi! Thanks for being here! Thanks for all your help!" the President said cheerfully, adding a few words about the importance of it all, and then she began shaking the worshipful hands presented by the Ambassador. As she worked the crowd

("Hi! How are you? Good to see you. Where you from?") the line of people collapsed and reformed and split again. Diana and Brian maneuvered backward, trying to escape notice, but it was not their week: suddenly The Hand was extended to Diana and the Ambassador nervously announced, "Diana Ventura, one of our young Economic officers."

"Diana!" smiled the President. "Are you the one--?"

"Yes, Ms. President, I'm the one --"

"No," coughed Brian, "excuse me Ms. President, I'm the one."

"Brian Brown," sighed the Ambassador. "Consular officer."

"How sweet," said the President, looking from Brian to Diana and back again. "And I'll tell you a secret," she added, leaning close. "I hate that cat. But find it anyway -- Pat's driving me crazy! I'll be so grateful."

And then she was gone.

"She'll be 'so grateful' that you'll get double promotions or something. Maybe." Brian spoke cautiously, afraid either to dash hope or encourage illusions.

"Or a job in the White House," she added dreamily.

"I hope it's not real soon." He looked at her with all the pain of separation in his eyes.

"Not likely," she answered harshly, the pain of disillusion in her own. "That cat's probably dead by now, flattened on the Corso d'Italia or somewhere."

Brian kept a respectful silence as they walked slowly through the tree-lined parking lot. *That lousy cat! It's somewhere at this moment. Where? Well, Where would I go?"* He gazed around the ever-illuminated Embassy grounds. Cats lived here, of course, and in the Villa Borghese; he'd seen them sunning themselves in the Forum and on the battlements of San Angelo Castle. But where would a tomcat go to find an inexhaustible supply of cats all compact together? He had only to pose the question to answer it.

"Diana!" he said urgently, "The Coliseum!"

The wizened little guard stepped out of his smoke-filled cubicle looking as though he'd been jealously guarding the place since it opened. As they explained their mission his face changed from irritation to puzzlement to amazement: *i signori americani* wanted to enter the Coliseum now, four hours after it closed, to look for a cat?

"I'm sure the Foreign Minister will be most grateful," coaxed Brian.

"But," asked the guard, "What about the Minister of *Beni culturali*, eh? The Foreign Ministry doesn't control the Coliseum, does it?"

"Oh, Brian," said Diana hopelessly, "that would take weeks! And how could he have come this far anyway?"

Diana discouraged was more than he could bear. "Just give me a minute, O.K.?"

She let out a long sigh and shrugged.

Brian smiled wanly at the guard, opened his hands in a Roman gesture and put an arm gently on the man's shoulder, leading him a few feet away.

"*É la fidanzata,*" he confided. "My girlfriend's heartbroken about the cat."

"Ah, *poveretta!*" the old man sighed, looking towards her. "And so beautiful!"

"Yes," agreed Brian sadly. "But she can't think of anything until we find it."

The guard began nodding and moving his right hand jerkily up and down, emitting a low melodious sympathetic eeeehhhh. "*Va bene,* just this once -- but don't take any of the stones!"

They stumbled down the walkway to the small viewing area and despite their urgency, stopped to gaze: the moon shone on half the interior of the ancient stadium, only to leave the other half in deeper obscurity; the effect was almost musical.

"Beautiful," said Diana. "But how will we see a cat?"

"Look," he whispered. "There's one -- and another. And two more . . ."

"Oh."

On the ruins of the ancient tribunes, and in the niches along the wall, and the ledges, and on the stairways which had led festive Romans to their seats 1800 years before, small vague spots of darkness moved cautiously, or jumped, or calmly sat and licked themselves. All cats are gray in the moonlight, too, but at least they differed by size. None looked half the size of Inscrutable.

"He could be out there and we still wouldn't see him," complained Diana. "And if he's down there," indicating the blackness of the ancient subterranean passages long since exposed to the sky, "we'll never find him -- even if he's here!" She seemed on the verge of sobbing. Brian's own heart ached. He determined to be brave for both of them.

"Wait," he said. "Just wait."

Weary Diana leaned lightly against him as they searched stones old beyond imagining, bathed in moonlight as ancient as time yet always newly arrived to show lovers in softest light. Perhaps they'd find their prize, perhaps not, but for Brian this moment mattered more than a cat or a career.

"He's there," she said quietly, breaking the spell.

"Where?"

"On the other side, climbing up from the . . . locker rooms, or whatever."

"Where . . . ah, I see him."

In a stadium full of cats there was no mistaking his heroic stature and majestic stride, as if he were a waking lion eager for Christian breakfast. Most of the other cats edged quickly away from him, like waves pushed from the bow of a warship, but some sat and looked back in coy admiration. Inscrutable studied them appraisingly.

"You go that way," whispered Brian, pointing with the gunny sack. She nodded.

It wasn't easy picking a route through the maze of ruined walls and bleachers. Sometimes they had to jump carefully over chasms through which lions and gladiators once passed and then look quickly again for their moving prey, for Inscrutable had set his own course toward a gray shadow ten feet above him, which jumped from one stone to another wailing as Inscrutable closed. Brian willed the Roman cat to cooperate, to occupy the single-minded visitor just long enough.

Their progress described a strange clocklike dance to the cat's singing as Diana and Brian, the hands, moved around the face of the Coliseum to Inscrutable's noon. The female reached the outer wall as Brian and Diana closed behind the Siamese, which seemed to lose patience.

Brian got the sack ready. The Roman cat could go no further: Inscrutable and he crept forward together -- and then she jumped, somehow elevating herself ten feet onto the top of the wall! Brian cursed but Inscrutable seemed neither surprised nor concerned; surveying the distance casually, he jumped himself, landing within two feet of the other. The low wailing grew urgent.

Brian moved quickly now -- what need caution when all could be lost within minutes? Throwing the bag to Diana he began climbing, digging his fingers into the ancient wall, scratching for footholds. The rough bricks raked his face and legs, opening wounds suffered at the Residence, but he ignored the pain, concentrating entirely on the wall's edge that jerked steadily closer.

He could not see the cats but their raucous love song guided him truly and well. He slipped, and made a racket catching himself; then listened breathlessly. Still the wailing. He sighed in relief: One more foothold and his head would pop above the wall.

He calculated the cat's location in relation to his head and hand as he stood up. Picture it in your mind, he thought, like shooting freethrows. Push up with the left leg, right arm around the cat, tuck him to your side, and scramble down, pluck him in the sack. Right. He took a deep breath and pushed up.

The two cats looked at him in surprise and disgust but their shock provided his opportunity: he punched his fist through the air and wrapped it around the Siamese in one motion, then felt for the foothold below. But Inscrutable was no longer in shock.

They really do go for your throat!, Brian thought in amazement. *Even a damned housecat*. He turned his face away and held as tightly as he dared--Inscrutable dead solved no problems. But the ungrateful beast reached across somehow to draw deep gouges in Brian's left hand, causing him to lose his grip, and his balance. He landed backwards on something hard and jagged; despite the pain spreading from head to hips to feet, he rejoiced that he could now use two hands to control the demonic thing on his chest.

"Put him in! Put him in, quick!" Diana rushed to his side, holding open the sack.

Brian rolled to his left, pushed Inscrutable deep into the sack and let go as Diana closed it. As he squeezed his hands out the cat got in some final shots at his fingers.

"We did it!" Diana announced happily, tying the sack tight.

"Yes," he moaned. "We did!" As he sat up he heard strange clicking noises in his neck and back.

"You son-of-a-bitch," she smiled, holding up the sack which twisted and hissed.

"*Ooo-ahh!*" Brian groaned, standing up shakily.

"You O.K.?" she asked, putting down the sack.

He gazed at her gratefully. "Sure," he said. "Just a scratch."

"Hey, good job getting the cat, Brian. Thanks."

All the pain disappeared. It dissolved away like the heat of a summer's day when sun gives way to moon, and soft sea-borne breezes chase away the dust and noise of noon. She had seen; she knew; she cared. He looked on her face in the moonlight and thought it wonderful that he had found future happiness in this site of ancient suffering.

"Diana," he said hoarsely, "I'm just glad . . . just glad I could do it. For you."

"Oh," she said, surprised, looking at him again in a different way.

"I mean, these have been the happiest hours of my life, Diana. Being with you, I mean."

She continued to gaze at him, her lips parting slightly. The moonlight reflected off her alabaster forehead and in her blue eyes, and her dainty hand shone as white as the stone on which it lay. He could contain himself no more: placing his raw rough hand gently on that white hand, he choked, "Diana, I think -- I know, I'm . . . in, like, love. With you."

Her eyes flashed recognition, or perhaps confirmation, as if she saw now clearly what she felt but did not understand before. A smile played on her lips as she watched his hand gently slide up her arm, as if he had awakened some primal memory deep in her modern woman's heart, and transformed fond fantasy to frank proud desire which demanded satisfaction here and now without fear or guilt or shame. She pulled her hand gently away from his, pivoted slightly toward her right, and then swung back gleefully to punch him in the mouth.

Brian fell back over a low wall and sprawled among the ruins, staring vaguely past Diana frozen in triumph, toward the upper wall of the Coliseum, at cats. They returned bored glances: cruelty was nothing novel here, nor harsh justice, nor the decline and fall of empires.

Memorare in Autumn

Grandpa's funeral pretty much filled up Immaculate Conception, and that's a big church. Grandma would have been proud (God rest her soul), and so was I even though it felt weird hearing these prayers for Daniel Malone. That's my name too, so it was scary in a way, and something else. I mean, knowing that I would walk out and see the sun again made me feel pretty lucky. And sort of envious: I hoped that someday I'd get as much satisfaction from my funeral as Grandpa must be getting now. And not just for the friends either: he got the last laugh all right. Mom worried that people would blame the family for not looking after him like we should. But anyone who knew him knew that he never listened to anybody, except Grandma, and after she died he got real stubborn -- and even more, once he got sick.

He went once to Doctor Haley and once to one other guy and never went back, even though he felt miserable some days. He never said what it was, exactly, just that it was "too disgusting to talk about." Some kind of cancer; we knew that from the appointments Haley made for him, but Grandpa never kept those. He just sat home, hardly even going out for walks anymore which was one thing he kept up after Grandma died; now he never played tennis down at the park like he'd done for fifty years, or went to the bar or to baseball games. I guess he was depressed, and I couldn't blame him. And I wasn't even sure what I thought about it: I liked Grandpa a lot and didn't want him to die -- he was just about my only friend, at least in the summertime -- but from what my Mom and Dad and the others said, it was just a matter of time no matter what he did. They said you have to try -- that he had to get past "denial" even if it didn't do any good.

Aunt Nora and my Mom got bills for those appointments Grandpa never kept, and they'd nag him for wasting money and he'd answer, "Who asked you to make any damned appointment anyway?" He started coming over for dinner less and less, and looked more tired and pale every time we went over there. He was never a real big man, though he was strong from all that construction work, but now he seemed to disappear into his recliner chair, and you could see the pain in his eyes.

Finally Mom decided to try something else. So one Saturday when she dropped me off to mow his lawn -- Dad was off on another business trip -- she asked,

"What if Father Melrose comes to see you?"

"Not time yet," he answered glumly. Before Grandma died, he used to sort of grin when he talked about how old they were and how their days were running out. He turned back to the television but he wasn't really watching the baseball game. His glasses were on the coffee table.

"Well maybe he could talk some . . . he's a nice priest. It would do you good to talk to him."

"Bernadette, just drop it," he said sternly, adding, "I don't need any priest yet. When it's time for confession and all that, I'll let him know."

"Why wait 'till . . .: I mean, he's your pastor. You don't need a special reason to see him. Except there is a reason. You're sick. It would do you good."

Grandpa snorted. "Might do me good if we had a pastor like Father Burke, God rest his soul. The man knew how to drink and tell jokes. I'm not looking forward to the last rites from the sort we have now -- or do they even do that anymore? Maybe they play you something on the guitar."

"Well I just think it would be nice."

"And I don't."

"Well I do."

He stared real hard at the television.

After she left, I sat down and pretended to watch the baseball game. Grandpa put on his glasses and really did watch for a while. "Look at that!" he said, when the Orioles turned a double play, but it sounded fake. I wished I could think of something to say.

"Well, Danny," he asked when the side was retired. "You going to mow that lawn or not?"

"S-Sure, Grandpa." I got up and put on my Orioles cap. "I wish you weren't s-sick, you kn-kn-know?"

He looked at me and sort of smiled. "Then I could mow my own lawn, right?" He always talked to me like to anybody, even when I was little, like I didn't stutter.

"Yeah, that t-too," I laughed, and started for the door.

"Danny," he said, "it's the way it is. You get old and sick and die, and in the meantime you mow the lawn." He looked like he might say more but he didn't. He wasn't smiling anymore either.

One thing about my mother, when she gets an idea in her head she wants to do something about it right away, as if waiting would mean the idea wasn't really a very good one after all. As I was putting away the lawn mower, Father Melrose drove up, then sort of jogged over to me. He was wearing a Washington Bullets warmup outfit and looked almost like a player. They say he was pretty good in high school. He didn't look much like a priest but then again, he almost never does. But he's all right, I guess -- everyone always says he's a really caring priest. We even joke about it: when someone says "Who cares?" about anything, my Dad (when he's home) or my sister Kate or I answer "Father Melrose cares -- he's really caring!"

I brought him in the house and tried to get away but Grandpa wouldn't let me. "Danny! Get that bottle of whisky in the kitchen -- surely you'll have a drink, Father?" Everyone knew Father Melrose didn't drink.

"No, thank you," said the priest. "Or just some mineral water, or a soft drink. Whatever. And are you sure you should be drinking just now, Dan?"

"Never more sure, Father."

I could hear them talking as I got the things from the kitchen (I finally found some Coke at the back of the refrigerator). Father Melrose said he had come by because he was concerned, and the family was concerned, and they all cared about him. Grandpa said "Yes, thanks a lot," and "how 'bout them birds, Father? I didn't think they could play this bad. They might as well go on strike -- they're sure not going to the World Series!"

Father Melrose pretended to be interested in baseball for a minute, but by the time I set the Coke in front of him he was talking about our obligation to care for the body as the temple of the Holy Spirit.

Grandpa came right back: "Cemetery's full of temples, so I don't guess the Holy Spirit needs any one in particular. So what are your Bullets going to do this year?"

"Dan, what finally happens to us is in God's hands, but He/She expects us to do what we can to take care of ourselves."

Grandpa groaned and shook his head: he could never stand the way Father Melrose and some of the others talked. He used to get into big arguments with the various lay people who seemed to do more and more at Mass, but he never argued with the Pastor. He was too old-fashioned for that. "You don't talk back to priests," he'd say. "Doesn't matter how dumb or rotten they are, they're still priests."

"And when there's nothing to do, Father, what then?" He turned toward the window as he said this, and the sun reflected off the bald spot on his head.

"We never know that," said Melrose confidently.

Grandpa sighed. "Well thank you, Father. I appreciate your coming by."

But Father Melrose didn't move. "Dan," he said quietly, "it's your *obligation* to try. Just to give up is like saying you don't have faith that God can heal us -- as if you didn't believe in the countless miracles God has worked over the centuries."

Grandpa took another sip of whisky and shuddered. "Oh I have faith in that, Father, that God and the Virgin can work a miracle if they want. But we're a long way from Lourdes. And besides, you can't expect them to keep us all around forever. Got to make room for the young people."

"God knows what . . . He has to do, Dan. We're not supposed to decide that. We're just supposed to ask for help."

"Just ask for help?"

"And take reasonable measures."

Grandpa stared at Father and sort of smiled, like he'd just thought of something. "All right, Father. I'll think about it."

"You will?"

"Sure. 'Reasonable measures,' just as you say."

"Good. Good for you, Dan. Bernadette will be so glad. All the family will."

"Well, well," Grandpa answered. "Now how 'bout your Bullets?"

Father Melrose called Mom that night and she was feeling pretty proud of herself; first thing Monday morning she made new appointments with the doctors: one on Thursday morning and another on Friday. She insisted on taking him herself and we were surprised that Grandpa didn't even argue because he always drives himself everywhere. Mom took this as a sign he was starting to accept things. But he just outsmarted her. Thursday morning she found a note on his door:

> Took a trip. Don't worry. Neighbor's feeding the cat. I'll send you a postcard. Key's in the usual place. Love, Gramps.

Mom got on the phone with her brother and three sisters and them all mad and worried and they weren't much relieved when the first postcard arrived two weeks later from Lourdes. It was a picture of the fountain and the Basilica behind and Grandpa wrote,

> Whole lot more fun than the hospital, but almost as expensive. They speak English funny here, but lots of nice people. How's Mary's lumbago? [That's my Aunt Mary, with the bad back.] Lit a candle for it -- hope it works. Cost 50 cents. Love, Gramps.

So now the family was really mad and everyone agreed he had gone totally senile and wondered if there was some way the U.S. Embassy could put him on a plane and get him home but my cousin Louie the lawyer said you'd need a court order and all kinds of things and forget it. So we'd just have to hope he came to his senses soon. Except Aunt Mary: she said her back *was* better and maybe a couple more candles wouldn't hurt.

The next card was from Fatima, a picture of the Virgin in the Grotto, and dated a week after the first. It said,

> Dollar worth a little more here and I'm getting more for it than I would from Haley and that crew. Regular UN here, even met a guy from Bari. [In Italy -- that's where his mom came from.] Ireland next. Love, Gramps.

Then there was one from the Marian shrine at Knock. The last one, from Dublin, said "See you soon."

And sure enough, three days after the postcard arrived and just before Thanksgiving, Grandpa called Uncle Jack from New York and said he'd be on the 7:45 flight. Mom and Dad went to the airport too, and Aunt Laura, so they could start badgering him right away and when they got home they were all in a bad mood, even Grandpa, though he tried to act cheerful during the Welcome Home Dinner. Mom tried to stop nagging, for a while, but then at dessert she mentioned how hard it had been to get new doctor appointments for him. He didn't say anything for a while, just stared at his plate. Then he sort of smiled and said, "I'll bet!"

He didn't keep the appointments, of course, and wasn't even home when we went to get him (Mom thought he might be less obnoxious if I was there) and Mom called up the doctor to see if he'd gone there by himself and then apologized because he hadn't and Yes, she knew she'd have to pay anyway. When Grandpa showed up in a tennis outfit she just about went ballistic.

"Just what in the name of God do you think you're doing?" she asked. "Have you no consideration for anyone else at all? Do you know what I've been through all morning? And where have you been -- playing tennis at your age?!"

Grandpa smiled but you could see he was trying not to get mad and he looked kind of silly, with that smiling-mad face and his thin legs sticking out of old tennis shorts too big for him and that little old wooden racket.

"Well, I thought I'd hit a few balls with Carl. Been a while, but I still got it!" he said, demonstrating a smooth backhand. "Would have beat him, if I could get to his first serve."

Mom said she was just too disgusted for words and that she was washing her hands of the whole thing. "If you won't listen and just want to die, well there's nothing I can do about it!" she said. Actually, she sort of sobbed it, but Grandpa wasn't impressed.

"Good!" he said. And more gently, "It's all in God's hands anyway, Bernadette. And the Virgin's. Everything's going to be fine, whatever happens. But you're a good girl to care so much -- even if you are as stubborn as your mother, God rest her soul."

Well, of course Mom didn't wash her hands of it and talked about it with her sisters and brothers almost every day on the phone, and at a family dinner before Grandpa arrived, they grilled Louie about how you get a court order and he said it would take a lot of time and money and there were no guarantees. Aunt Laura asked why they had spent all that money for law school if he couldn't even make somebody go to the doctor.

"S-Seems to me he looks a whole lot b-better," I said. But I guess people never listen to kids no matter how old you get. (Kate looked at me and shrugged, though, like she agreed.) But they pretty much dropped the idea, especially since no one wanted to see Grandpa hauled away in a straitjacket anyway. Still, at dinner if Aunt Mary or someone said "God helps those who help themselves," or something; he'd smile and answer, "That's the truth." One time Aunt Laura nudged Uncle Mike until he said, "if you loved us, you wouldn't make us suffer like this." Grandpa looked at him for a minute and asked, "You remember how it was with your mother, toward the end?" Everyone shut up.

I thought I had him once, when I was over helping with the storm windows: I told him he couldn't expect God to heal him just like that because God has lots to do and we're supposed to take care of our own bodies. But he came right back:

"I know that. God's busy -- that's why we have the Virgin. Besides, I didn't really ask her to take care of it, just to do whatever was best for everyone if it was all the same to her, and that I'd really prefer to go fast when my time comes, and have a nice day. That sort of thing. Asked Saint Joseph, too."

But what finally got the family off his back -- that is, what got them to give up -- was when Father Melrose changed sides. Or maybe he just gave up too: he went over there by himself one time and they had a long talk and afterwards Father told the family he didn't think there was any point in nagging Grandpa anymore, and "Anyway, I'm not sure he's not right." Afterwards Mom was really mad for a while. "As if I didn't know my father was 82 years old! Where do they find these priests anyway?" But she got over it, especially since Grandpa seemed to be doing all right.

He didn't look real healthy but he must have felt better, because he took up skydiving and hang-gliding and even golf, for a little while ("at my age I don't have time to search for lost balls"). He took me to an Orioles game and then not just me, but some kids that Father Melrose suggested. One of them, Damian, said he was going to get me some pot but he never did. Grandpa said it wasn't their fault these kids didn't have fathers to teach them to keep promises and stuff. He started hanging out at that soup kitchen the parish runs, and got Karen and me to help him deliver meals to old people who can't get out, but he still found time for tennis and skydiving and in July he made his first solo flight in a hang glider. Mom shook her head and sighed and said, "He's going to get himself killed," like you might say, "It's going to rain." And she was right.

The hang-glider club said it really wasn't his fault, that there was this really weird air current or something. Mom stopped crying long enough to say again, "I *told* him so!" And she sort of smiled and added, "Wait 'till I get my hands on him!" Before she started crying again. But she seemed better after the funeral, after seeing all those people she didn't even know but who had nice things to say about Grandpa. And being busy helped: she took over Grandpa's chores at the soup kitchen. Myself, I still miss him sometimes but at least I still see Damian and the other guys a lot, and when Dad's home he picks up where Grandpa left off -- taking us to ball games or for pizza or something, and he got a hoop for the driveway where we play basketball. No one mentions Grandpa much anymore, but sometimes I wonder if forgetting can't be another way of remembering.

More Than A Tourist

Gladys wouldn't admit she had lost her way; the very thought of admitting it vexed her. She had come once before to this old Colonial section of Quito with her son and daughter-in-law, stumbled across the ancient stone pavement while gazing at the huge white church of *La Merced,* and visited the gray Jesuit parish of *La Compañia* with the twisted columns and the statue of Saint Ignatius in front. She would recognize those, and other churches whose strange melodic names she couldn't remember. She knew that the huge plaza with the bus stop couldn't be far away. But these funny little winding streets closed her in like canyons and she couldn't orient herself by church steeples or by the arid-looking mountain ranges to the east and west, or by the huge statue of the Virgin on a hill to the south or by that big mountain -- what did they call it? *Copitaxi?* Something like that.

When she turned back the way she thought she had come, she faced two even smaller streets that went up and down. She was tiring fast under the sun that burned down through the high thin air -- nearly 10,000 feet -- especially when one carried twenty extra pounds. And so many people! She couldn't help bumping into them but she would smile and they would smile back, many of them looking up at her as if she were a marvel. For the first time in her life she felt tall, but that didn't help with directions. Still, she'd find her way. She'd find her way home today and come back again tomorrow and lose those twenty pounds with the exercise. That would make her cardiologist happy.

"Maybe down that street," she thought, wiping her brow with a tissue and pushing her glasses back in place before turning into a lane which looked as though it would wind back towards the plaza, or at least to one of the big streets that led to the center of this Andean capital.

Who would ever have thought she'd come to Ecuador? She had hardly even heard of the place until her son was assigned here, and insisted she visit. So here she was and it had been wonderful, though she couldn't help thinking how much more wonderful it would have been if Neil were with her. But he wasn't, and if being a widow meant taking airplane rides by yourself, well, she'd just have to do it.

They timed her visit so she'd arrive just as the grandchildren went on a week-long Easter vacation, and John had taken a week off from the Embassy where the people were so nice to her, and they had explored the old city and gone to little villages north and south of this beautiful mysterious *Quito* -- Gladys always thought that was a funny name -- and she'd bought beautiful wood carvings and little Christmas figures made from bread dough, and a warm woolen *poncho* from the Indians who stood behind their stalls wearing those hats like she remembered American men wearing in the Thirties. The Indians smiled and gestured, pointing at their goods, each with a long braid of hair hanging down his neck. Even the women wore those hats, and they seemed so friendly. Gladys was sure it wasn't just because they wanted to sell you something; she always assumed that everyone she met was a friend just waiting to be introduced.

She knew she was naive; not everyone was nice. She had been shocked and angered to learn that Indians were still treated badly here, insulted and cheated and scorned and, until recently, even beaten. That information had cast this strange land in a darker light but it was nonetheless new and strange and wonderful, impossible to appreciate with hurried visits to one place after another. So Gladys had determined to give to the paintings and statues the study they deserved. John was back at the Embassy doing whatever important thing he did, and her daughter-in-law, Anne, was substituting for a sick teacher at the American School. Never one to sit and do nothing, Gladys had put on her carefully-ironed blue dress and sensible shoes and the *poncho* and taken the bus by herself and really studied the statues and paintings in *La Merced,* seeing details she had completely missed before. Only after she began to weary of art, and decided to explore more of the old city, did her troubles begin.

The street grew more narrow, as if the two- story buildings on either side grew more neighborly as they moved away from the center. But where were the people? The street was almost empty. She stopped and sighed and thought about taking off the *poncho*. The mornings were so cold that she had needed it; now the temperature had shot up and she was too warm and could feel her heart racing. But you have to take *ponchos* off over your head and that would displace the carefully colored brown hair she had combed so precisely before leaving the house. Where would she find a mirror to fix it again? Better just to walk more slowly.

Ahead of her the houses grew even closer and lower. What to do? Anne had given her a card with the bus number (37) and their address, *Eloy Alfaro 1644*, telling her "If worse comes to worst, just get in a taxi and show them this." But there were no taxis. Her heart began to beat even faster, not just from the heat and thin air but from incipient panic. She told herself to calm down. The doctor said to avoid stress. She leaned against a building and breathed evenly for as long as it took to say an *Our Father*, a *Hail Mary*, and a *Glory Be*.

She wandered cautiously another hundred feet and found a lane that turned sharply to the right. "I'll just try this," she thought nervously. "And if it doesn't work I'll go back the way I came."

It didn't work. The lane turned only to expose three smaller lanes. She turned back and saw two streets converging behind her. The buildings began to float before her eyes; her heart beat frantically against her ribs and she was afraid. "Mother of God!" she prayed, "get me home!"

"Got to ask someone," she told herself amid the dizziness and panic. She couldn't speak Spanish, but she could show the card with the address, or say *plaza* and gesture and they'd understand. "Of course," she thought . "Why didn't I think of that before?"

Turning a corner she saw an open door with a crowd of Indians in front of it, all short with jet-black hair and mostly white pants and colorful *ponchos* and the ever-present fedora-style hats. Most had cups in their hands and were eating some strange-looking food. So there was a party going on. "Forget the address," she thought as she approached them. "I'll ask for the plaza." But before she could ask anything of the men who stood at the doorway they moved aside with mixed expressions of surprise and curiosity, bowed slightly, and seemed to invite her into the house. One of them said something she couldn't understand at all. She smiled at their evident good will but was embarrassed to go into someone's house to ask directions. Only their renewed gestures and the apparently earnest words of an older man drew her on. She stepped through the door, from the bright glare of noon into obscurity and the low buzz of incomprehensible conversation, and of weeping.

As her eyes grew accustomed to the light her smile faded, faded together with the conversation. She looked around the small low dark room and saw, first, children scurrying from sight. Then her eyes settled on a group of women who stared at her from the floor, or from the few chairs arranged around a small white casket.

"Oh," she said. "Oh." Automatically, she made the Sign of the Cross.

An old woman approached her and cautiously touched her hand and murmured something in a low voice. Gladys understood only *Señora* but let herself be led to the small open casket in which a girl of four or five years lay, dressed in white.

The woman said something in that strange language but the gestures, pointing to a young woman who wept quietly on one side and then to the child, explained everything. Gladys looked from the child to the mother and the grandmother and back at the child and mother and without thinking went softly to the younger woman, crouched down, and embraced her. The tears running down her cheek mirrored those of the other.

Gladys found herself sitting on a chair someone had provided. The conversation was renewed. Between daubing at her eyes with a Kleenex, Gladys carried on her own conversation with the young woman. She looked at the casket, held up five fingers and raised her eyebrows. The young woman shook her head and held up seven fingers. Gladys looked again at the child. *Poor thing! Poor thing!*

"What's her name?" Gladys asked, quite forgetting she'd not be understood.

"Marisol," the woman said. "Marisol Maria."

Someone put a cup in her hand and Gladys sipped without thinking, hardly noticing the foreign bitter taste of whatever it was. Nor did she refuse the food, a sort of taco tasting vaguely of corn, that a woman brought. Before she finished it she had learned that the mother's name was Juanita, and the grandmother Juana, and she had met Pedro, the girl's father. She met Tómas, and Anna Maria, and Mercedes.

As she left she fumbled in her purse and pulled out most of the *sucres* she had, money John had given her with an explanation she couldn't remember about exchange rates. "Please," she said, offering the bills to Pedro. He shook his head and smiled sadly. Gladys insisted: "Everything costs money. Even . . . " She nodded at the casket. The man again shook his head, and Gladys looked around the room and with one hand pointed to children who stood half-concealed behind their mothers. "For the others," Gladys said and thought hard until she found the word she wanted, one that Anne had taught her. "For the *niños*," she urged. "*Niños.*"

She understood Pedro's *gracias, gracias,* as she gratefully handed him the bills.

Gladys understood that the man who led her back to the plaza was named Enrique, and that he was Marisol Maria's uncle. He waited at the bus stop until she had boarded Bus 37, and waved as she left. On the ride home, gazing at the ornate churches and the dusty trees and white houses with red tile roofs, and listening to the chatter of Spanish and that other language of the Indians, she found it all familiar.

Bus No. 43

"Ohh . . . *damn!*" Janie cursed the gust of wind which had just destroyed her careful alignment of umbrella and bags, allowing rain to pour again over her cloth hat and down her matted hair into the sacks brimming with groceries. Would everything be destroyed before the bus showed up?

"*Ma dov'é?*" she asked no one in particular. The old man next to her smiled sympathetically and said "It is where it is. This is Naples."

Sunny Napoli, she sighed bitterly, remembering friends who had teased her husband and herself, saying they must have bribed someone to get this assignment. Even if Naples had a bad reputation for crime and traffic, the beauty of the bay and Vesuvius and the islands -- all hidden now by black low clouds -- was supposed to make up for it. But it hardly made up for waiting in the rain for a bus that didn't arrive, and that would leave her three long blocks from home, blocks where the cars on the sidewalk would force her into the puddles on the street.

Again she thought, "We need a second car!" And again she heard the landlord's warning: there was no garage for a second car; it would have to stay on the street where quick clever thieves defeat the most elaborate security systems. *Bella Napoli* indeed!

Her sodden bags began slowly to fall open. The wonderful smell of bread mixed with that of *salami* and *prosciutto* and three different cheeses. They might make the day worthwhile after all, if they weren't ruined. And the rich coffee should survive in its cheerful green and red can.

"*Signora*, is yours the 43? Here it comes."

"At last!" she thought, as the rear door -- the entrance door -- stopped precisely in front of her.

"*Signora,* permit me." The old man held the bags while she closed her umbrella, and then carefully handed them up to her on the bus. *"Grazie,"* she said, taking the bags carefully and squeezing into the aisle. Her right hand, under the bag, held her sodden ticket and she asked a middle-aged woman to cancel it. The woman looked at Janie's soaked hair and coat and smiled maternally. *"Poveretta!"* she said, pushing the soggy piece of cardboard into the orange machine and handing it back with the corner legally cut off.

"You're American?" asked the woman. The canceled ticket, and her accent, gave Janie away.

"Yes," she smiled, hoping it would excuse her. How to explain that she paid the fare not so much out of ignorance as cowardice, from the certainty that an inspector would board to fine her 10,000 *lire* the first time she did not pay? Many Neapolitans also paid, but just as many considered those who did so to be *fessi* -- foolish, naive people who didn't understand the way things worked, or who were too timid to defy the system which just benefits corrupt politicians anyway.

As the bus careened down Via Posillipo she kept her balance with practiced feet, anticipating curves and letting the motor warn her of acceleration. Braking was harder to anticipate but sympathetic passengers, seeing her problem, put out protective hands against disaster. After the next stop, someone called to her from the front of the bus, pointing out an empty seat by the driver. She stumbled forward, thanked the man, and sat down just as the bottom of one of the bags begin to split.

"Damn! Damn! Damn!" she hissed, stretching her hand around to cover the opening.

"Signora! Che succede?" The driver looked over at her and smiled, his round face breaking into wrinkles which ran up his bald head. "What's the problem?"

"Everything's wet -- and falling apart!"

The man nodded sympathetically at the dismay in her voice. *"Un peccato!* But even the rain is beautiful! Where would we be without it, eh?"

She thought of her 45 minutes of beautiful rain. "Yes," she agreed politely, "but too much is too much. I was waiting for almost an hour."

The man nodded as if he had foreseen it all, as if he had stood there in the rain with her. "Giovanni and Michele, ahead of me, they both broke down. What can you do? These buses should all be shot, they're so sick! Look at those wipers! One doesn't work at all, and the other has arthritis!"

"Why don't they fix them?"

"Eeeh! Why not? You ask me why not!" And he rubbed his thumb against his fingers in the timeless gesture of money -- money wanted, money stolen, outrageous prices, bribes, but in any case money extracted from poor honest people like themselves. She smiled at the man's joy in expressing, in proper Neapolitan fashion, the wisdom and cynicism which made one superior to all life's dirty tricks. But now the other sack began to tear, and she could feel the salami trying to slip out.

"How am I going to get home?" she wondered aloud.

"Scusi?"

She repeated it in Italian.

"Eeehh!" the driver answered, indicating his profound understanding of her dilemma, of the injustice of it all. And then, "But *Signora*, where do you live?"

"Via Capri -- Vistamare Apartments."

He looked thoughtful as he pulled to the next stop. "Three blocks from the stop?"

"Right."

"We'll see."

She wondered what there was to see as she awkwardly gathered the sacks newly together; her stop would be next, and she began to stand carefully.

"*Signora*, stay seated! I'll take care of it."

The bus rocked to a halt at her stop and she began again to get up. "*Signora!*" he insisted, "Just relax!" And shutting the door, he swung the bus around the corner and picked a careful route through the parked cars on Via Capri itself. Creeping past an Alfa 164 he asked, "Why didn't someone steal that one?"

"Ma dove va?" shouted various passengers as he resumed speed on this unscheduled street.

"The lady's all wet," he shouted back. "And look at those sacks! Do you want the bread and salami and tomatoes all ruined? *Poveretta* -- she'd catch pneumonia in this weather! Besides, it's hardly out of our way at all."

The passengers found this argument unanswerable.

"Tante, tante grazie," she said as the bus stopped three steps from the apartment gate. "You're very kind. Really --"

"Non é niente, Signora! Don't mention it. The pleasure is completely mine! Be careful now you don't drop anything, and *buona sera!"*

She stepped off the bus to the applause of the other passengers. Despite her care she did drop something -- the salami slipped out just inside the apartment gate -- but it would take more than a slightly bruised salami to ruin the silly happiness she felt. Down the street the bus was carefully turning onto Via Sassari, which would take it back to Posillipo. From the rear window a young man was smiling at her, or with her, like a fellow-conspirator. She picked up the salami and climbed carefully but cheerfully up the stairs to the apartment, to her home in the most beautiful city in the world.

Pisa's So Near

Suntina set the pan on the stove quietly, careful not to awaken the guests. There was little danger of that, for these American cousins performed extraordinary feats of sleeping, wandering down to breakfast only after the sun was above the stable or even atop the cypress tree. She didn't resent such apparent laziness or even puzzle over it anymore: that's just the way they slept on their vacations to the old country. She thought only to make them comfortable; they were guests. Still, she wished they wouldn't come up with these strange ideas.

After eighteen years the new house, the *palazzo*, had become home, the corner of the world where Suntina Micheli knew intimately the inventory of the granary in the attic and the character of each cherub painted on the bedroom ceilings and, since her husband Nando installed the bathroom ten years before, the marvelous convenient sound of water rushing through bright chrome faucets and out through dark gurgling drains. Her gnarled feet knew the paths to the henhouse and through the garden and all around the small farm and all their particular depressions or stones or dangers, like the flagstone outside the stable on which ice formed on November mornings earlier than it froze anywhere else. Her hands had grown arthritic gathering eggs from one generation of hens after another until the rough henhouse roosts, too, were hers, and seemed to welcome her stooped gray figure each morning. What need had she to visit Pisa? Wasn't it enough that she had made the five-mile trip to Lucca a dozen times in her life?

On all the farm there was no place more home to her than the kitchen. She felt out of place in the seldom-used formal living and dining rooms that she cleaned weekly, but the kitchen was hers. Rising before anyone else she made coffee and warmed milk and laid out bread and jam for her husband and two grown sons, and after they had left for the fields she cleaned up the breakfast things and turned to the myriad other tasks which filled her life: washing the laundry at the cast-iron sink just outside the kitchen, killing and cleaning chickens and putting vegetables in the large kettle that dwarfed the small gas range.

71

Almost every summer she had another task: preparing delayed breakfast for guests who would eat quickly before rusing to drive off somewhere, to Florence or Siena or San Gemignano, places as foreign to Suntina as the America or Australia or South Africa to which these relatives or their parents had emigrated years before, fleeing the hardships of post-war Italy. This room had seen her pass from an energetic middle-aged mother worrying fretfully about still-unmarried children, to an old woman whose gray and failing eyes studied the color in her grandchildren's faces. And yet, despite all the ties to this kitchen and this *palazzo*, hardly a morning passed without her gazing across the fields at the other house, the one she had called home for so long.

It was much smaller than the *palazzo* and in fact not an independent house at all but one of four under the same roof, with bedrooms stacked between the ground floor and the granary—very like the home she had grown up in five miles away. Of course it enjoyed neither electricity nor plumbing when she arrived as a bride, but nonetheless had seemed huge and frightening and foreign to the shy girl. But with time she became part of this extended family living on fields bequeathed by generations past memory. She assumed the role of an adult, however junior in the hierarchical family, responsible for her kitchen and her bedrooms and the tiny sitting room in which she received her relatives from Tassignano. Soon enough, her own children were playing with their cousins in the dirt courtyard and jumping from the hayloft into the stack of sweet-smelling straw below. In this house she had not only become fully herself, but the house was woven into the woman she had become.

Even now she resented the Germans above all for taking her home and that of her brother-in-law during their 1943 occupation, forcing the extended family to crowd together in her father-in-law's house. The soldiers had done much worse things, like kidnapping men to work in Germany, and she had heard of atrocities in other villages, or rapes and murders. They were no atrocities in her village, but they took her home under her own eyes, and this belittled and demeaned her personally. When they finally left she came into herself again, though never quite with the old confidence. Ever after her daily prayers included the plea, "Protect our home."

So it had been hard to leave the old house when the time came, almost like a denial of her own prayers. But Nando was so excited about owning the 'palace,' and so pleased at his own financial cleverness in manipulating the price, that she had tried to be enthusiastic too. Nando was easily fooled. It took longer to fool herself, but with time pretense passed into reality and she really had found home again.

She smiled when these emigrants or their children talked of coming home to Capannori, as if a place can remain home when you aren't there anymore, and your bed and kitchen beyond the sea. Besides, they no sooner arrived then they left for a day or a week to see someplace else. But at least they returned: in the first war, Uncle Mario had left for someplace called Caporetto and was never seen again. And her cousin Giovanni had laughed from the train which took him to a grave somewhere in Russia during the second war that also took Mario Lucchese and Giorgio Tolomei and so many more. And now her niece Maria wanted Suntina to accompany her and her husband and children on a trip to Pisa, "just 50 minutes away!"

Suntina had laughed at the idea and repeated the old proverb: *Better death in the house than a Pisano at the door*. They had laughed too, though Maria insisted that the proverb was an old prejudice, that the *Pisani* were good people like everyone else, and besides, "*Zia!* How can you live all your life within an hour of the most famous tower in the world and never see it?" She didn't know how to answer such a question and merely repeated the proverb, which set Maria pleading again that Suntina let them do something for her, take her to Pisa and to lunch, in return for the hospitality they had received. When finally Suntina was convinced that they really did want her to go and were not inviting only from courtesy; the conviction made her worry that it would be rude obstinately to refuse a guest's request. With Nando also urging her to do so she had finally agreed, and tried now to imagine a day not devoted to lunch and laundry and shelling peas.

At first it was all right. As they drove down the village street she waved at neighbors who laughingly saluted the great lady out for a ride in her Mercedes. She identified each neighbor for Maria's two children, a boy and a girl who tried to seem interested. And once on the highway she could still identify most of the farms, explaining to Maria that the one with the untended fields had belonged to Giuseppe Lombardo who had died, and his sons were in Australia and now the land went to waste while lawyers did whatever they do. But after that she recognized nothing except, when the highway curved southeast for a moment, she could see the church tower of her native Tassignano. And then they were on the freeway in a foreign land.

Maria's husband, John, commented in his problematic Italian that it was all beautiful, *magnifico*, as he drove them past village after village with church towers strangely alike and yet unique, and fields defined by hedgerows and farmhouses both humble and magnificent. Suntina nodded agreement, though she saw something foreboding in the houses and barns which became subtly different as they traveled, with roofs or windows shaped somehow other than those of home. When they reached the edge of the plateau and started down, she was shocked to find the world grown so large, visible for miles and miles across fields and towns even to Livorno on the sea. She clung more tightly to the seat in front of her, not releasing her grip until they had reached the valley floor and turned off the freeway onto the slow clogged streets entering Pisa.

Suntina stared at strange stores and houses and at the wall that appeared on their left, a wall both like and very unlike the one which surrounded Lucca. She was dismayed by the Pisan accent in the voices that came through the open windows, an accent she had seldom heard except in imitation but one always associated with menace.

Maria and her husband continued chattering about the history of Pisa and its tower, about wars with Florence and Guelphs and Ghibellines, architects and soft soil.

Suntina nodded politely at it all, impressed at their knowledge but unsure what they were talking about and in any case more taken by the streets packed with strange people speaking in different languages, people of whom she knew nothing, neither name nor family nor village. Stranger yet, black men went from car to car in the stalled traffic, offering sunshades and postcards and statues of the famous Tower. Suntina stared at them, recalling vague memories of the first black men she had seen, Americans who came to the village after the Germans had left. They were not really bad boys, none of them, neither the Germans nor the Americans. But she had been glad to see them go.

"This is as close as we'll get," said John as he pulled into a parking lot outside the wall that enclosed the old city. A five-minute walk brought them to one of the medieval gates crowded with tourists of all races and descriptions. Maria commented that the Pisans had probably built the wall to keep the Florentines out, adding smugly "for all the good it did them." As they passed a group of huge blond people Suntina heard the unforgettable sound of German; holding her purse tightly she pushed ahead as fast as the crowd would allow.

Beyond the gate the crowd thinned out somewhat, and they made better progress through the narrow streets and the vendors. Suntina glanced right and left, marveling at the huge world of people and places that was not Capannori. And then suddenly the great square opened before them.

"Look, *Zia!* There's the Tower, and the *Duomo!* Isn't it beautiful? And look at the Baptistery there! Isn't it wonderful?"

Suntina stared. So that was what all the fuss was about. Yes, the Pisans' tower was pretty. Beautiful, except that the builders had made a mistake. And their huge church was beautiful too. And their little church.

"Yes," she said. "It's very nice. Now let's go home."

Rudolph's Gift, or
Why Naughty Children No Longer Get Coal in Their Stockings

Rudolph had two problems. The first was he couldn't think of a way to get revenge on the other reindeer. The second was that revenge probably wouldn't work. Not really.

He had arrived three months before and at first he had pretended that their teasing didn't bother him. He even added to the jokes about his nose ("Sometimes the light keeps me awake all night!") but that didn't help. They still didn't let him join in the reindeer games. Rudolph told himself they were stupid games anyway. Only Vixen had seemed like she even wanted to be friendly. She had sort of smiled at him once, as if she felt bad about the others teasing him; she even talked to him one day until she got teased herself for hanging around with the guy with the weird nose.

Subsequently, Rudolph thought of starting a fight with Blitzen, the biggest jerk of them all. The older deer was heavier and stronger but Rudolph was faster and might get in some good pokes with his shorter horns. If he could make Blitzen cry uncle, then Donner and Dancer and Prancer and the others would fall into line. They'd have to at least respect him as the new champion of the pasture and there wouldn't be any more teasing, not if he could show them who was boss. The flaw in this plan was that Blitzen was only *a bit* slower, while much stronger. Rudolph would lose any fight he started and provide them with another theme for their teasing. And even if he *did* somehow beat Blitzen and the others invited him into the reindeer games, they still wouldn't be his friends. They'd just joke about his nose behind his back. So he did nothing but brood. Sometimes the anger seemed to come up from his stomach like bile and he imagined insults or kicking Donner or anything that would make the others feel what he felt.

And what about Santa Claus? It seemed wrong even to think about insulting St. Nick but Rudolph couldn't help it. If the jolly old fat man hadn't himself quite teased Rudolph, neither had he stopped the others. In fact he had encouraged them, whether he meant to or not. So why didn't Santa do something about it now? The man who knew which children were naughty and nice had to know about his own sleigh team.

Several times each day Rudolph wondered why he even had to be in this herd of "elite" deer. It sure wasn't his idea. His father had come to him one day blubbering about this great opportunity that would bring honor to the family. Rudolph had been dumb enough to believe it but now he was pretty sure his father just wanted to get him away from their own herd because he was embarrassed by the nose that drew strange looks from uncles and cousins and neighbors even though no one exactly said anything about it. Only the youngest deer pointed and giggled. The others mostly looked away, pretending not to notice. It was a colossal embarrassment and Rudolph's sense of guilt made it worse. Had he obeyed his mother, he'd still have a regular nose like everyone else.

"Stay with the herd!" Mother had said with increasing exasperation every time Rudolph started, a year before, to wander off on his own to see what was among that stand of pines over there, or to go to the top of a hill to see what lay in the distance. He didn't want to disobey but curiosity would come on him like a hunger and he just had to know. Or, it was as if some other authority, even more important than his mother, was beckoning him. He'd be in the middle of the herd, scratching through the winter snow to find the grass beneath, or gorging on the tall sweet summer grass, when a strange uneasiness started in his chest somehow and then worked its way to his head and he'd look up and around and see some woods or notice how the river disappeared around a hill and just *had* to see what was there. Usually he wouldn't get far. For all her concentration on finding grass Mother seemed always to have an eye on him, as if he were still a fawn rather than a nearly full-grown buck. He began to plan.

On the summer afternoon it happened, the herd was grazing near a stretch of forest that ran beside a stream. Rudolph slowly worked his way to the edge of the group that had, in turn, slowly spread down to the bank of the stream. Chatting with Edelweiss and Pine and other friends when not chewing, he passed from one group to another until he was beside the swift-running water. He watched until his mother was turned the other way, her nose pushing aside the few inches of snow that had fallen the night before to reach the grass. Then he bounded over the stream and into the woods, not stopping until trees hid him. He turned to explore.

The place seemed strange but he couldn't say why. It was like any other forest where the herd had bedded down for the night. Yet it was different, as if it existed in a different time or held other possibilities than shelter or food in the form of tree bark or straggly bushes when the snow was too deep on the grass. He sensed there was something here, something rare and wonderful, and set out to find it.

In some places the thick trees provided a canopy that threw all into deep shadow. Where they were thinner the sun threw everything into bright relief. He kept heading east despite his sense that time was passing quickly and despite the clouds that suddenly rolled in from the west darkening the world. He didn't know why, but it seemed he just had to keep going this way. Then he came upon a fallen tree that might have blown down in a winter storm, or had died of very old age. Yet it couldn't have happened very long ago for its needles were still soft and green. Above it soared another tree, the only one for fifty yards in any direction. Rudolph felt a pang of sorrow and sympathy and imagined these two trees standing alone for years and now one was fallen and the other kept a mourning watch. Of course he knew trees were not reindeer and didn't have reindeer feelings. Nonetheless, he glanced up softly as if to say, "I'm sorry for your trouble."

As he looked at it a white light appeared in the highest branches, very small at first but rapidly growing stronger as its color shifted from white to blue and green and pink and red and white again, making the pine look like a huge Christmas tree. Rudolph had seen the Northern Lights often enough but they were in the sky, not in a tree. He stood transfixed as the light, brighter and brighter in the afternoon shadows, lifted from the tree and seemed to spin as it floated out and around the tree in widening circles until it came at last to Rudolph, brushing his nose and then floating back and up. It stayed still for some moments. Rudolph had the absurd feeling the light was watching him or, even more absurdly, trying to tell him something. But he heard no words, not even in his mind, and a moment later saw the light shrink to a smaller but very brilliant point and then fly away to the east so fast that he could follow it only for a second.

At first Rudolph was too amazed to think anything. Then he imagined the light had gone back to the other lights, wherever they stayed when they were not putting on a display. But it had gone in the wrong direction. Can a light get lost?

Reindeer can get lost, he thought suddenly. Now he had no interest in exploring any more forest or hills or rivers but wanted only to rejoin the herd. It was when he turned to retrace his route that he noticed his nose emitted a soft yet strong red glow.

His mother began to scold him angrily when he leapt back across the stream and joined the deer who now closed quickly around him. "Don't you know we've been worried sick looking for you?" she began. As he drew nearer she stopped scolding. "What happened to your nose?"

He had no explanation. He might have described what he had seen but it sounded incredible even to him. The rest of the herd gathered around, looked at him and each other and him again with puzzled eyes.

"Well," said his Aunt Moss, "whatever it is will go away. Must be something he ate."

But it didn't go away. Eventually his father described the great opportunity that would bring honor to the family. He made it pretty clear that refusing the honor would bring disgrace. So Rudolph was the one sent to fulfill Santa's request for a suitable young deer as a candidate to join the elite sleigh-pullers.

Santa had said nothing about the nose when he saw Rudolph, and the elves and other reindeer followed his lead. But when Rudolph was inducted into the Training Unit of the Reindeer Corps, receiving the power to fly via a complex ceremony he could barely follow, Santa stared at the nose and chuckled and said, "We'll never have any problem finding Rudolph!" The others took this as permission. When Rudolph joined the others in the pasture beneath the toy factory, Blitzen began the teasing at once: "Hey, check out the schnozz! You been into the eggnog already or what?" The others followed suit, vying to invent the most cutting remark. Rudolph hoped they would have had enough after a day or two but they didn't.

Even the two other new recruits, Slapdash and Playful, got into the act, as if they could speed their acceptance among the others by joining in the ridicule of "the Schnozz."

Rudolph was grateful for the training because the joking stopped when the recruits were taken aside and made to concentrate on the lessons. Almost every day one of the Regulars would lecture him and Slapdash and Playful on the logistics of delivering Christmas presents, how to avoid tangling the harness, or the various commands Santa would shout and how they must respond, how to fly in formation and plant your feet as you land on a roof and a dozen other things they would have to master before they could be promoted to the Regulars. Rudolph thought most of it wasn't really that difficult and suspected they had the trainees go through all these drills just to keep them occupied until one of the Regulars got too old for the job.

A class consciousness existed, or a dividing line between working and learning reindeer. Yet they all mixed together, playfully butting heads or chasing one another through the snow. All but Rudolph. Maybe some of the others would have let him in but when Vixen looked as if she was about to invite him, Blitzen ambled over to spoil it. "You like the Schnozz? That's nice! You can have a red-nosed fawn!" After that Vixen kept her distance though she would glance at Rudolph now and again as he stood apart by himself, sympathy and shame in her eyes.

Rudolph soon learned to stay as far from the others as he could. Doing so provided only a brittle sense of self-respect, not nearly enough to hold off the rising tides of sadness and anger. Resentment increasingly seemed like his only friend: it was there when he awoke and remained his companion all the day. It grew despite Rudolph's resistance, spreading out to include the father who had sent him here and the mother who hadn't kept a closer eye on him that day by the stream.

On the First Sunday of Advent Mr. and Mrs. Claus and the elves put up the crèche between their house and the pasture, with Mary and Joseph and the shepherds and sheep gathered around the manger that would remain empty until Christmas morning. Training classes grew less frequent and stopped altogether by mid-December as the Regulars met with Santa to plan routes yet again, or with the elves to double-check the gear. Santa seemed everywhere at once, and increasingly irritable and demanding as he consulted the Doll House Division or Factory Five (nicknamed "the Pirates' Den") that produced Nintendo games and popular music CDs. He checked inventory and production schedules against his summary of Letters to Santa and went to the Coal Mine office with a list of naughty children and berated the manager for not yet having enough coal to meet demand. The manager in turn berated his shift foremen, who complained about lazy elves or muttered about obsolete equipment that should have been replaced years ago.

Despite or because of the hectoring all seemed ready by Christmas Eve. The sleigh was fully loaded. But there was no sense of relief or achievement or anticipation. Instead, Santa and Mrs. Claus and the managers and elves and reindeer peered nervously at the fog that had begun floating in that morning and now limited vision to a few feet. It might have been the very embodiment of gloom rather than just its cause as it seeped through the factories and the pastures. It so disheartened everyone that none had the spirit even to tease Rudolph, who cautiously joined the other reindeer at the top of the pasture near the house, setting aside his anger in order to enjoy this interlude of indifference if not acceptance. They noticed him of course. How could they fail, when his nose marked his place unmistakably and its light let them see one another while all the land about lay in gray-black darkness? But they said nothing. Humor – even the now-venerable teasing of the Schnozz – would have been out of place.

"It's got to lift," said Prancer bravely. "We've never had to cancel because of fog!"

"First time for everything," sighed Donner.

It didn't lift. Silence prevailed; none dared ask what would become of children so cruelly disappointed. The fog only grew thicker as departure time grew closer.

The reindeer looked up when they heard the *crunch* of boots in the snow. And then a shout: "Rudolph!" It was Santa's voice.

"Here!" Instinctively he moved toward the voice. The glow from his nose now showed, if dimly, the figures of Mary and Joseph and off to the right, the sleigh heavily laden with sacks of toys and candy and coal.

"Indeed you are!" Santa emerged from the gloom into the wide circle of rosy light. "Ha! I said you'd be easy to find!"

The reindeer laughed as usual.

Rudolph looked from Santa to the others and back thinking, *the old fool still doesn't get it.*

"We need you and your bright nose tonight. I'm told you've done well in training and even though you haven't quite finished, you're ready. Will you guide my sleigh tonight?"

Rudolph again looked from Santa to the other reindeer and felt an answer welling up inside: *No way! You and this company of jerks can fly into a mountain for all I care!*

He hadn't said it aloud but Santa seemed to hear all the same. "It's Christmas," he said.

There was fear in the old voice, and Santa's eyes were troubled as if he already saw Johnny Brown and Maria Jimenez and millions of others looking into empty stockings with pained disbelief.

Rudolph resisted the appeal of voice and eye; he began formulating a sarcastic comment about his nose and how they'd be embarrassed to travel with him. As he did so the nose glowed more brightly, shifting very subtly from red to pink and throwing out suggestions of green and blue. The blue seemed to reach even further through the fog, banishing the dimness around the manger that would soon receive the Child. Rudolph had often asked bitterly why this strange thing had happened to him but had never really sought an answer. Now he felt certain the light, whatever it was, hadn't changed his nose just to bring him humiliation. A sarcastic refusal would indulge his anger, and sarcasm tempted him like something sweet and ennobling. Resentment had not been a good companion but it had been his only one and now a perverse loyalty to the perverse companion was on the point of winning. Then he looked more closely at Santa. The jolliness was gone. Rudolph gazed on a frightened and desperate old man. He shut his eyes for a second and, when he opened them, said quietly,

"All right. Thank you."

Santa breathed a heavy sigh of relief. The other reindeer gathered around Rudolph and began dancing and chattering.

Blitzen gave him a friendly head-butt and said, "You da man!" Vixen nuzzled his neck.

"Bless you," Santa said, again with a jolly face on him. "I owe you one. Anything I can do for you, just ask."

Rudolph stared for a moment at the crèche and then at the sleigh. "Unload the coal."

The old man looked surprised, then frowned. "I know I owe you one, but this is unheard of. What do we give them instead?"

"Toys, tangerines – whatever."

Santa sighed. He was a man of his word, and reluctantly ordered the elves to offload the coal and replace it with the good stuff. But he looked hard at Rudolph and asked, "Just like for the good children? Is that fair?"

Rudolph's shiny nose turned from Santa to the crèche and back. "Fair is for another day."

Same Mother, Same Father

The phone rang as I walked through the hallway on my way to breakfast. I picked it up without thinking -- usually I didn't answer the phone, and for good reason. A woman said something I could not understand at all except for the one name, *Armand.*

"Armand, *pour vous*," I called into the kitchen.

Our combination cook and housekeeper appeared immediately, his habitual smile in place. I left him to deal with it and went eagerly to the breakfast of rich coffee and tropical fruits Armand set out most mornings: pineapples and bananas and mangos. I heard the one-sided conversation and understood none of it, though I recognized it was in Armand's native dialect from the north of Togo, rather than the local Ewe language of Lomé. In a few moments he appeared in the door.

"*Perdon, Daddi*," he said softly, his smile replaced by an expression not so much of sadness as of acceptance. "That was my big sister. My little sister has died, and I must go."

"Oh," I said, pushing back the chair and adding in my uncertain French, "*Je suis désolé.* Very sorry. Your little sister?" I wasn't sure how to ask just what he meant by "sister" since I had learned, after a year working in a country where polygamy was common, that *sister* or *brother* in French and English substituted for a host of local words specifying anything from brother to half-brother with the same mother, with the same father, to paternal cousin to someone not related by blood at all, but who lived in the same house. Sharing a house, I supposed, created a family connection and that was why he referred to me as *Daddi* and to my wife as *Mamá.*

"Yes," he answered. "*Même mére, même pére.*"

That was definitive, and described the closest of relationships: same mother, same father. "But what happened?" I asked. "How old was she?"

Armand shrugged. "Twenty-nine," he answered and then, concentrating, added, "Or twenty-eight. *La maladie.*"

The malady. "Diphtheria?" I asked. There had been something about an outbreak of the disease in Daipong. Diphtheria appeared there almost every year, after the rains. But I'd been told *maladie* often meant malaria and sometimes AIDS.

Armand shrugged again, as if the question had little interest for him. "Maybe," he said. "I will be gone for five days, or perhaps a week. Is that all right?"

I assured him it was, trying to put a good face on it. In fact we had missed Armand a great deal when he had left two months before to attend ceremonies on the first anniversary of his father's death. We had another two employees, also inherited from the previous tenant of the house, but for all their merits, neither Laré nor Sarkon could cook. Still, we would manage for a week without Armand: my job at the Embassy involved several meals each week at some sort of diplomatic function. But I worried about his making that three hundred-mile trip.

The only transportation was provided by tiny Japanese mini-vans built for eight passengers, into which the drivers packed a dozen or more people and stacked baskets of fruit or wickerwork or chickens on the roof before racing along the crowded two-lane roads as fast as the small engines permitted, dodging potholes that made the roads look as though they had been bombarded. Stories of accidents with eight or ten people killed were common. But I knew he had to go. No one who has spent any time in Togo can fail to appreciate the importance of the funerals that consume not a few hours but days and weeks and even years as various anniversaries are remembered.

He left that afternoon; we missed him. It was not so much for the meals he would prepare since my wife enjoys cooking and does it well, but because Armand was such a happy presence in the house. From his arrival in the early morning until he returned to his own wife and children in the afternoon, he combined unvarying cheerfulness with a hard-headed practical approach to whatever problem presented itself, from dealing with the fish-monger who appeared on Mondays and Thursdays, to fixing leaky pipes or squeaking doors. He came to mind as we took our walk in the evening.

It seemed there was always a funeral in the neighborhood. The sandy street would be covered by a temporary tent for several days as hundreds of people -- relatives, neighbors, people with roots in the same village, co-workers -- would enter the house of the deceased to pay their respects, and gather under the tent for songs and remembrances. Usually the body would be carried to a nearby church or mosque for a funeral before the procession carried it to the cemetery. But with or without Christian or Moslem services, the funeral always included deep-rooted local customs: dancers, chants, the recalling of the deceased's ancestors whom he would now join, father and mother and grandparents even back to several generations. We had attended one such funeral that ended at the cemetery with the priest saying Catholic prayers over the grave as dancers performed nearby, invoking God in a different language. We imagined Armand at such a ceremony. He had told us, rather proudly, that his family had been Catholic for three generations.

We thought of him also when, walking through the streets and exchanging greetings with men who sat playing cards at a shaky table, or women selling rice which they cooked over a wood fire, or the children running everywhere, we found the same friendliness and interest in us which seemed to go beyond the courtesies which you might find in Seattle or Naples or Quito. Very soon after arriving in Lomé we understood that people all up and down our street knew who we were and, despite the very great differences between us, seemed to greet us on our strolls as part of their neighborhood, at least for the present. They seemed very much to live in the present.

Probably we just didn't understand and were twisting what we saw into our own terms. We certainly didn't understand the common language, *Ewe*, that was more in use than the official French I had learned to mangle. But it seemed that these people included us in their world in a way we had not experienced before. "Seemed" is the operative word because Togo was foreign to us in ways that Latin America and Italy, children of Europe, never were. I think you're not really at home in a country until you acquire enemies, or at least people you dislike, as well as friends. In Togo we discovered only friends, or friendly people. The newspapers carried daily accounts of the deadly sins and we heard horror stories about the fate of discarded wives and exploited children and government corruption. Yet somehow we couldn't see egoism and arrogance as we could in other countries. I saw only innocents and wonder if I was guilty of something worse than naiveté.

We were pleased and relieved when Armand reappeared a week later, as cheerful as ever. "Everything was done," he said of his sister's funeral. "Everything is all right." And we were left to muse again on local attitudes towards mortality.

We had thought that what seemed like bland acceptance of death was due to its frequency. Life expectancy is not very great in Togo and many funerals were smaller, centered around a small white casket. Since death is so common, we speculated at first, maybe it's not considered remarkable or shocking. But that notion was contradicted by the very elaborate funerals and visible mourning we could see and hear. Of course death was a big thing, something that justified great expense to bury relatives properly. I finally inferred that their resignation was rooted in an absence. In the U.S. we often bring resentment and anger and surprise to funerals, blaming God or fate for an early death or any death at all. That did not seem the case in Lomé.

In time, we realized that we had heard the answer almost every night, that it had been there all along. A house not far from our own had a sign, "Church of the Spirit," and the singing that began in the afternoon often went on to the small hours. On Sundays, we never had to wonder when Mass began at the nearby Catholic church, for the singing and the drums announced it for blocks around.

Or the answer was on the taxicabs with their "Jesus Saves" bumper stickers, and in the Moslem men bowing toward Mecca in afternoon prayer and in the Masses at our local church which went on for more than two hours as the people sang or listened to very long sermons in the local language, danced unselfconsciously up the crowded aisle to place a few coins in the collection, and enthusiastically sang the "Our Father." In sum, God filled day and night for the Togolese, all the days that had been and all the nights to come. Their reverence for ancestors proclaimed that the dead never leave us, that their spirits are as real as the trees in the forest or the wind blowing dust down the street. If this sentiment has pagan roots the Togolese nonetheless fit it admirably into the Christian concept of God who holds all things in being always.

About a month after Armand's return the apparitions began. Three children, refugees from the chaos in far away Rwanda and resettled in Tsevié, a village thirty miles north of

Lomé, had claimed to see the Virgin and announced forthcoming apparitions. Then hundreds and thousands of people claimed to have seen the same thing, an image of the Virgin in the sky. The Church was prudently skeptical of these visions though even the village priest confirmed that he too had seen something. Of course there is such a thing as mass hysteria, and plenty of charlatans have taken advantage of the credulity of simple people, so we had our doubts. And so did Armand, but he wanted to see for himself.

The next, and last, apparition was to be late on a Thursday afternoon. Armand left shortly after lunch and when we saw him the next morning his usual cheerfulness was overlain by a newfound tranquility.

"Did you see the Virgin?" my wife asked.

"Oh yes, *Mamá* I saw something. In the sky. Something beautiful."

My wife and I looked at each other. Armand was a sensible, practical man. It was hard to believe that he had been taken in by a charlatan, or had simply let his imagination run away with him.

"Well," I said. "That's wonderful. I wish now we had gone with you."

"Oh yes, *Daddi*! You should have come." He stopped and thought a moment, and then said quite seriously, "*Meme mere.*" The same mother. And looking at us both he added with a gesture to include us and himself and all the neighborhood and more, "*Meme mere, meme pere.*"

Secrets

Father Giobbe checked his wallet to be sure he had the twenty dollars for the chips. He did, with seven dollars to spare. Maybe this would be the night ~~he~~ he'd finally get lucky and come home with his own money and more from the monthly low-stake poker game with seminary friends from forty years before. Usually he came home with nothing except relief that, under their home-made rules for inflating the value of chips with never-to-be-paid IOUs, he could lose no more than twenty dollars. He'd just have to remember to limit himself to two drinks. With a third he began to play stupidly. But he'd been advising himself of this for years and wistfully regarded his inability to follow his own advice as just another failure, one to add to all the others..

Just as he entered the rectory hall the bell chimed. He opened the door of the rectory and peered through his thick glasses to see a young man in a dark suit looking up at him.

"Father Giobbe?"

"Yes . . ." He hoped the man didn't need anything that would ruin his poker night.

"Sorry to bother you this late, Father, but my grandfather . . . well, he's in real bad shape. Doctor says he probably won't make it through the night. He wants to go to confession."

"I see." He shuddered as the November wind blew rain and maybe even a few flakes of snow into his face. "But please come in. It's cold out there!"

"Thanks."

Father Giobbe closed the door, confident this wouldn't take long. "Every hospital has a chaplain on call," he said. "The simplest thing would be to call him." Under the overhead light the caller looked older than his voice; there were a few wrinkles in his dark face and around his brown eyes and he seemed slim despite a small paunch that pushed out his coat.

"He's not in a hospital, Father. Said he wanted to die at home, in his own bed sort of. Know what I mean?"

"I see. Is he a parishioner here at St. Stephen's?"

"*Nonno* don't belong to no parish, Father. Not really. Hasn't been to church in years except for weddings and funerals. Said he wanted an Italian priest and someone mentioned you."

Father Giobbe sighed, both for his lost poker night and for his own undeserved reputation as "an Italian priest." If his very limited Italian let him understand that *nonno* meant *grandfather,* it would be wholly inadequate to hearing a confession. "Does your grandfather speak English?"

"Oh, yeah. Sure. Came to New York when he was like five years old or something."

"That's good. I'm afraid my Italian is really poor. Give me a minute. And, excuse me, what's your name?"

"Louie . ." The man paused for a mini-second. "Louie Esposito."

The priest returned to his office, took a stole and a small bag with holy oil from a drawer, and called his old classmate Mike Hurley to say he'd be late for the game.

"We'll miss your money. What's up?"

"Sick call. See you when I can."

"Great excuse, Giobbe. Always with the excuses."

He smiled as he hung up. He had earned a reputation for offering excuses in the seminary because he was always screwing up something. His friends never let him forget it. But it was all in good fun. Except for the guys who had left the priesthood – about half of them – his classmates remained close friends. All but Ryan – make that *Bishop* Ryan – who had never fit in anyway, had never seemed to want to. No, Ryan had concentrated on memorizing the opinions of his superiors on all subjects political, theological, sporting, or anything else. Giobbe told himself to get off it and avoid Envy, the stupid sin. OK, Ryan was a jerk but maybe he was a saint, too. Lots of the saints were people Giobbe didn't think he'd want to hang out with. He went back to the hallway and as he pulled on his faded black overcoat asked Louie for the address. "I'll meet you there." He wrapped his thick wool scarf tightly around his neck. Of late he seemed to have lost his ability to fight off colds, along with most of his once thick black hair.

"No, no, Father. It's kind of hard to find. I'll give you a ride and then bring you right back."

"But I won't be coming back here. I have an appointment—"

"No problem. Wherever you want to go, no problem. OK?" Louie Esposito said this in a way that didn't invite discussion. Father Giobbe felt a vague sense of apprehension but dismissed it and shrugged his agreement. He could get a ride back from the game with one of the guys.

Outside, Louie led him down the street to the next block where a dark van sat, with someone in the driver's seat. He slid open the side door and held out his hand, inviting the priest to enter. As he did so Giobbe noticed there was someone in the third row but could barely see him in the dark. As soon as he sat down Louie jumped in, sat beside him, slid the door shut and said "Go!" to the driver.

Father Giobbe thought he shouldn't have dismissed his feelings of apprehension so readily. There was something fearful about the situation. He wanted to dispel it. "Are you all family?" he asked, surprised to hear chuckles in response.

"You might say that," said the driver.

"Uh, Father, hope you don't mind but there's something we got to do. Just as well you don't know just where *Nonno* lives."

"What? Why not?"

"It's complicated. Anyway, we'd like you not to see nothing. Better for you, you know what I mean. So we're gonna put this bag over your head. Don't worry about nothing. Ain't gonna hurt you. Just safer that way."

"A bag?" Anger began to mix with apprehension. "That's not going to happen. Forget the bag or find another priest!"

The last words were muffled as a soft bag of some sort – it felt very smooth, almost like silk – came down over his head. "Sorry, Father, but you're the guy. I know it ain't regular, like, but it's the way it's gotta be. Just relax."

Relax! He was being kidnapped and they told him to relax? Yet strangely enough he did begin to relax as he recognized there was absolutely nothing he could do about his situation. Argument was pointless and struggle even more so.

I'm in the hands of the damn Mafia! he thought. An habitual voice inside his head said *No, you're in God's hands, as always.* He prayed silently and grew calmer yet. Now it was clear enough: some old Mafia goon was dying and wanted to unburden himself, while his "family" wanted to keep everything as secret as possible, didn't want him to tell anyone where he had gone. It all made horrible sense. He just hoped that this sense was, in fact, the truth, and they had no other plans for him.

He tried to guess where they were going, listening for whatever he could hear over the *thump-thump* of the windshield wipers. His suburban parish was far from the old "Little Italy" section of New York where Italian priests were once plentiful. But there were still a few such immigrant priests so why had they picked him? He'd probably never know. Maybe it was more convenient: he was sure they were *not* heading into the city. They would have been on the expressway by this time and traveling faster. Maybe the old dying *Mafioso* lived on an estate on Long Island or someplace, like Don Coreleone in *The Godfather.* Eventually they did speed up, but not for very long. Then he felt himself pulled this way and that as the car went down a twisting road.

It slowed and he heard the crunch of gravel beneath the tires. The car stopped and he heard a motor come on and something rattling. The car moved forward slowly and stopped. Again the motor and rattling – *a garage door coming down.* That was easy to guess.

"Here we are, Fadder." The voice behind him belonged to the man who now pulled the bag from Giobbe's head. He looked around at the large garage. Though it was huge, big enough to hold four or five cars, it was empty but for the van.

"This way." Louie gestured toward a door at the far end of the garage. It led to a wide hallway and past an enormous kitchen and then to a foyer with paintings on the wall and thick carpets on the floor. A wide stairway ascended to a balcony that ran around three sides of the large area. As he climbed the stairway Fr. Giobbe tried to study the paintings he passed – they looked impressive for their elaborate frames if nothing else – but could see few details in the soft dim light. He did recognize the subject of one of them: Saint Stephen, the first martyr, being stoned to death. It might have been a good sign. Or not.

He followed Louie down the balcony until he stopped in front of a tall door, knocked on it softly and then pushed it open. A nurse stood up from a chair near an enormous bed and came over to the two men. "He's awake," she said softly. Turning to the priest she added, "He dozes on and off but never really sleeps very well. Maybe he will. After."

"Please God." He took off his overcoat and scarf and laid them on one of the matching chairs, picked up his bag and said, "Please wait outside. I'll call you if I need you."

"We'll be right outside, Father." Louie managed to make it seem like a warning.

When they had left Fr. Giobbe pulled the chair the nurse had used closer to the bed and sat down, staring at the old man who lay with his head on a thick pillow, strands of surprisingly still-black hair, lightly mixed with gray, running in various directions. Beads of sweat worked their way slowly through the deep wrinkles on his forehead and the face that seemed, with its strong chin and bushy eyebrows around coal black eyes, to project strength and authority despite the gaunt cheeks and the fact that the man seemed small – maybe the size of a large child – in the oversized bed.

"I'm Father Giobbe from St. Stephen's. I understand you want to confess."

"Good to meetcha, Fadder." The croaking voice also had more force than seemed possible from a dying man. "Yeah, I wanna confess. I'm Giovanni . . ." The old man hesitated.

"I don't need to know your name. Surely you remember" – the priest smiled softly – "your First Confession, how it's supposed to be anonymous even if you knew the priest knew who you were as soon as you spoke?"

"Yeah." Giovanni chuckled softly. "Long time ago. "Thought the stuff I confessed was a big deal. What did I know?"

"Would that our sins never got worse than those when we were seven!" Giobbe smiled. "But they sure do – yours and mine and everyone's. Shall we start? You remember the words?"

"Yeah, I think so."

After Father Giobbe had kissed the stole and put it on he turned slightly to his right and stared at the wall so as to provide some semblance of anonymity to the penitent. He made the sign of the cross and asked the man to begin.

"Bless me Father, for I have sinned." Giovanni said the words almost with smug satisfaction for having remembered them. "It's been . . . Christ, I don't know how . . . .long it's been since my . . . last confession!" His breathing seemed to grow shallower and he paused for breath every few seconds.

"Months? Years?"

"Years!" he responded quickly before going on as if it were important to get the details right. With frequent pauses for breath he said, " I think maybe the last time was after my first hit – that would have been in . . . ." He frowned. "1947? Something like that. Yeah. '47, when the Yankees beat the Dodgers in seven. I remember thinking maybe I was doing Pete a favor since he was such a big Dodgers fan and was feeling lousy. Anyway, I went but it didn't seem like there was no point because once you're in, you're in and when you gotta whack a guy you gotta whack him so what's the point of confessing it when it's your job and you can't quit?"

"And have you quit now?"

"Oh yeah! Look at me! I don't do that stuff no more."

"Go on," the priest advised. "You need not got into all the details – I'll ask if I need to know something. Just recount all your sins as you can remember them."

Father Giobbe tried not to look shocked as he heard of one murder after another carried out by Giovanni himself or at his order, of fire-bombing stores where the owner had resisted paying protection money, of bribing judges and politicians ("is that a sin, Father? I mean, isn't that on the judge or the senator?"), beating people with a baseball bat to compel payment or obedience, operating prostitution rings, controlling a drug distribution network and killing competitors. Giovanni wasn't sure that was a sin and laughed hoarsely as he asked. "I mean, you whack a slimeball dealer, that's like a public service ain't it?" The priest sternly told him it was nothing to joke about. Murder is murder. "Yeah, guess so. OK, I'm sorry about that too."

The old man's memory seemed intact, even if his penitence was doubtful. Some of the murders he recounted as if remembering good times, or as if his self-respect had demanded someone be whacked. When he finally finished, with the financing of a robbery at JFK Airport two years before, he seemed to relax. Giobbe could not tell if Giovanni relaxed because he had unburdened himself of his sins or because he had told a life story of which he remained rather proud.

Father Giobbe felt grateful for the seal of confession. He had heard enough to help the police send murderers to jail and break up crime rings. He would gladly do so. Or, he'd think he should do so even though he'd almost certainly be murdered himself. But since he had was firmly forbidden from revealing anything, he need not face that choice. He had only to give Giovanni salutary counsel. "Before I give you absolution you must promise to do what you can to make restitution to those you have harmed."

"Restitution? How can I do that when the bastards are dead?"

"Their families may need help. The police need help in solving crimes. You must do what you can to stop these things from happening again. You said you stopped going to Confession long ago because there was no point when you knew you would kill again. Same thing now: you can't expect forgiveness if you intend to let all the evil you've begun just continue."

"So what can I do, Father? Tell the guys to cut it all out? Ruin the family?"

"Yes. It won't be their ruin. It might lead to their salvation."

"Gotta do that, huh?" He breathed softly and thoughtfully. "OK. I'll tell 'em to cut it out, go straight. Drop a dime and help the cops clear up some things. Can't guarantee they'll do it, you know."

"I know. But you'll be facing God shortly. It's not about what others do but what you do while you can."

"Gotcha."

"For your penance, say the rosary every day for a week. If you can. Pray for the people you have wronged, and for the strength not to fall again into sin. Now make a good Act of Contrition."

As Giovanni began stumbling through the words he hadn't said in decades Father Giobbe began the absolution: ""May the <u>Almighty God</u> have mercy on you, and forgiving your <u>sins</u>, bring you to life everlasting.—"

"Wait a minute Father. Can't you say it like they used to, like what I remember? You know, the Latin?"

"The rite is in English now."

"Yeah but it don't seem the same. I mean, I'd feel better if it was like when I was a kid. Seemed like the words meant more somehow . . ."

The priest didn't think it an outrageous request. If the dying man really wanted to come back to the Church, why shouldn't it be the Church he remembered,? Anyway, this wasn't the place or time to explain liturgical changes. But could he remember the Latin? He concentrated, trying to call up seminary studies that had been rendered obsolete shortly after he was ordained. Slowly they swam to the surface. "*Dominus noster Jesus Christus te absolvat; et ego auctoritate ipsius te absolvo ab omni vinculo excommunicationis et interdicti in quantum possum et tu indiges. Deinde, ego te absolvo a peccatis tuis in nomine Patris, et Filii, et Spiritus Sancti. Amen.*

Giovanni finished his Act of Contrition and said, "Thank you, Father."

Giobbe glanced at his watch, not entirely surprised to see that forty minutes had passed. He'd never heard a longer confession. Getting up he took Giovanni's hand. "God keep you."

"You too, Father. You think I'm gonna be OK now? With God?"

"Nothing is more certain than God's eagerness to forgive sinners. If you are truly repentant you have every reason to hope."

"But you don't give no guarantees, huh?"

Giobbe sighed. "A guarantee from me wouldn't mean much. But you have Christ's promise. You want a better guarantee than that?"

"Guess not." Giovanni struggled to sit up and then fell back. "Do me a favor, Father. There should be a rosary, or a dozen of them, in that drawer there." He pointed to a small cabinet on the far side of the bed. "The wife, she was a good woman, never missed Mass or nothin', had tons of them."

The priest opened a drawer and indeed found a ton of rosaries. He gave one to Giovanni who kissed the crucifix and began to pray.

Giobbe put on his overcoat and opened the door to find the nurse and Louie, who looked up from his watch. "All done, huh?"

"All done."

"He didn't fall asleep on you?" the nurse asked.

"No, he didn't." Giobbe wondered about that, for the man was utterly worn out.

"OK, Father. I'll take you home."

They retraced their steps to the garage, where the priest was surprised to see three men, one of them very large, looking at him from folding chairs arranged in a semi-circle. A fourth chair sat facing the other three.

"Have a seat, Father. We have to talk a bit before you go." This from the large man, whose black suit seemed more elegant than those of the others.

"About what?"

"Please, sit down." As if to enforce the point, Louie put a hand on Giobbe's shoulder and guided him to the chair.

"The old man looks pretty bad, doesn't he? It's sad but – well, our days are all numbered." The large man spoke clearly and well; he clearly had more education than the others. "The problem is, he was always one for keeping things to himself. There are things he knows that we need to know. So I'd like you to tell us what he said."

"You know I can't do that."

"Yes, of course. Seal of the confessional and all that. I know it's irregular but the welfare of a lot of people depend on it. For instance, the business a couple years ago – you know what I mean?"

Giobbe guessed it was about the airport job but said nothing.

"Come on, Father. We need to know who his contact was. And we aren't going to tell anyone you told us anything." He smiled. "We have our own version of the seal, call it *omertá*.

You wouldn't be the first priest to cooperate. And you know, we take care of the people who cooperate. I know you've got money problems there in St. Stephen's. We could help. Or, you ought to have a nice new car to replace that junker Civic you've been driving forever."

"Every parish has money problems. But help on these terms, no thanks. It's not going to happen."

"You know," sighed the man, "we also take care of people who *don't* cooperate. It's really in your best interests to help us out."

"Again, you know I can't do that."

"Maybe you don't think I'm serious." Now there was no trace of a smile as the man nodded to Louie who moved in front of the priest and put a revolver to his forehead. "We don't like to kill priests," the large man warned, "but as the old man always says, *Ya gotta do whatcha gotta do.* So why don't you tell us before St. Stephen's has to look for another priest?"

Instinctively he recoiled from the cold barrel on his forehead; it slipped down only to the bridge of his glasses and followed him until he could lean no farther into the chair. *They can't be serious!* he thought, but the dark scowl on the large man's face told him yes, they could and they were. But it was too incredible to believe he could die here, in the garage of some Mafia don from the movies – and as a sort of martyr, a 21st Century Saint Stephen! It was too absurd! In a moment the man would say he was just kidding, some sort of twisted Mafia humor.

"I'm not kidding, Father. You got ten seconds. Ten . . ."

Thoughts raced through the priests head almost too fast to register. Maybe I should tell them? If God can forgive all the murders of Giovanni upstairs, surely He'd forgive a violation of vows – it wouldn't even be a sin so much as just cowardice, or weakness.

"Nine."

He didn't want to break his vow, would never choose it! It was being forced on him! *All right, I'm weak, I'm afraid – yes, I know I should be strong but I don't want to die!* Surely that should excuse his failure?

"Eight."

He was needed at St. Stephen's: there were no priests to replace him! He had stayed faithful all these years when others had left or, like that jerk Ryan, avoided parish work as much as possible while climbing the ladder to bishop.

"Seven."

A mocking voice swam into his head: *Good excuses, Giobbe.*

"Six."

Excuses. Have I learned nothing?

"Five."

The wonderful justifications collapsed into blackness. *This is where God has put you and you look for an excuse.* That thought did not pass away like the others but remained as a certainty and grew: *No excuses. Keep your promise. Keep your promise.*

"Four."

For their souls and his own he crossed himself, shut his eyes, and prayed aloud, "Oh my God I'm heartily sorry for having offended Thee."

"Three."

"And I detest of all my sins because I dread the loss of Heaven and the pains of Hell but most of all because they offend Thee . . ."

"Two."

"Who art all good and deserving of all my love. I firmly resolve . . ."

"One."

"With the help of thy grace to confess my sins, to do penance, and to amend my life. Amen."

In the quiet that followed he wondered if the shot had been fired and this was the silence of death. But no. He sensed the others in front of him. He opened his eyes. The revolver was no longer there.

"You're OK, Father," said the big man. "We had to be sure."

"You mean you were never going to kill me?" He couldn't prevent his voice from shaking, or his shoulders.

"Only if you answered wrong. You talk to us, you'd talk to others. Have a nice evening. And this is for your trouble, coming out on a night like this." The large man leaned forward and pushed several bills into the pocket of Giobbe's overcoat.

Louie led him to the van. Inside someone put the bag over his head again and they backed out of the garage, turned down the gravel driveway and onto a highway.

"Where'd you wanna go, Fadder?"

"Go?"

"You said you had an appointment."

"I did?" He thought a moment. Of course. The poker game. He laughed despite himself, it seemed so long ago, so far away, so unimportant and yet so wonderful. "Right. You know where St. Rita's is?"

"I know," said the driver. "That's where Mike's funeral was."

After a few moments Louie said, "Guess you take that secrecy stuff serious, huh?" Louie asked.

"Yes, I do."

"Good for you."

"I can tell you this. Your *nonno* took confession seriously. At last. You shouldn't wait so long."

"Hey, time comes, I'll do what *Nonno* did."

"You sure you'll get the chance? Lot of guys in your business don't die in bed. You might think about that."

Louie was quiet. After a moment he asked, "So what you got to do at St. Rita's?"

"Got a poker game there. Bunch of old friends."

"Hey, now *you* better be careful. Can lose a lotta money in those."

"Not tonight. I'm feeling lucky."

The New Neighborhood

Walter Carroll stumbled up from the basement, carrying the box of flags on his ample belly. Abigail looked up from the newspaper on the kitchen table and peered over her reading glasses. "You'll never get your money back," she said.

"You wait," he answered confidently. "You just wait. It'll be like the old days."

"I hope so," she sighed, pushing strands of gray hair aside and turning back to the paper. "Good luck."

Outside, Walter checked to be sure the door was locked, as the experts advised, then stood under the flag fixed to his own door frame and looked around at the cul-de-sac into which they had moved two years before. It was quiet and very pleasant, this collection of vinyl Colonial homes that mirrored each other, just what they had wanted in retirement. "Too quiet," he thought sometimes, echoing the old movie line: the place was almost deserted during the week, and on weekends no one seemed to have time for neighbors. Not like when he was a kid. Maybe this would help.

Next door, John was rolling his lawn mower out of his garage. Walter hurried over before his neighbor could start it. "Morning, John!"

The tall austere man looked up like he was irritated at the interruption, and returned the greeting formally, correctly, like he did everything. Even the pressed work clothes he had on looked like they'd been designed for weekend gardening, for all that they seemed out of place on this intense executive.

"Got to do it, eh?" Walt asked, looking at the mower and the lawn.

"No one's going to do it for me."

"Well, before you do, let me sell you a flag."

John looked at the box. "Why do I need a flag?"

"Tomorrow's Flag Day! I noticed last year most people didn't have one, so I went and bought a bunch. Give it to you for cost -- eight bucks, including the flag holder. See, comes with a staff and even screws for the holder."

John shook his head solemnly. "Don't need one."

"Of course you need one! Everybody needs one on Flag Day -- don't you remember how it used to be, the whole street in the old neighborhoods would by flying Old Glory!"

John still shook his head. "I work about seven months of the year to pay taxes -- federal taxes, business taxes, state taxes, municipal taxes, county taxes, license taxes, Social Security. Damn government owns me already and I don't see why I should celebrate it."

"Come on, John -- " The fixed look on the other's face convinced Walter it was hopeless. "Well, O.K.," he sighed."Thanks anyway."

The next house was empty, for all that it was Saturday. And at the one after that the door was opened, finally, by a woman who spoke no English. She called in some strange Oriental language and three men appeared, but between the bunch of them they didn't have enough English for Walter to explain his purpose, even with gestures toward the flags. They smiled a lot though, and bowed as Walt left.

He found the next neighbor just jogging home, a red sweatband holding her long brown hair in place. She looked at him suspiciously but grew thoughtful as he made his pitch. "Yeah," she said when he finished. "Why not? At least a woman has a choice in this country. Eight bucks? Just a minute."

While he waited Walt wished he had skipped this house. This wasn't the idea at all. Not that there was any point in arguing with her -- he'd just get depressed. He had to swallow before he could say "Thank You" when she returned with the money.

The young man at the next house smiled and said thanks, but he already had one. Walt didn't ask why, then, he had not put it out last year. But at the next house, the one on the main street, he was greeted warmly by a fat bearded man in a Harley-Davidson T-shirt who was working under the hood of his pickup.

"Damn right," the man said. "Been meaning to get one," and he yelled through the garage, "MABLE! BRING ME EIGHT BUCKS HERE!" And turning back to Walter he smiled and said, "Still the greatest damn country in the world, least 'till *them*" -- nodding down the street and across the street -- take it all. I had buddies die for that flag." The man sniffed, and both men observed a few seconds silence until a spectacularly fat woman appeared with bills in her hand.

Crossing the street, Walter rang the bell of the only black neighbors. The man who answered looked at Walt suspiciously through tinted glasses. Walt explained, but the man's gaze shifted: he watched over Walt's shoulder as the fat man across the street began to fasten his flag-holder to the wall. "That guy buy one?" he asked.

Walter looked back. "Yes, he did."

"Then I guess I won't. Thanks anyway," he concluded coldly.

The box was getting heavy and Walter set it down at the next house, the one with all the kids whom he'd overhear speaking English to one another, and Spanish to their parents. Three smaller boys were in the yard and ran to look at the flags, enthusiastically endorsing the idea of buying one. Two of them ran into the house shouting *"Mama! Mama! Compremos una bandera!"*

Two short dark women appeared, looking at Walt fearfully. His efforts to explain proved both useless and needless: they could barely understand him, but the children explained it all. One of the women disappeared into the house and returned with eight dollars that she handed to him reluctantly; the other continued nervously to watch. "You don't have to," Walter said guiltily, but doubted that this was translated accurately.

The young couple at the next house were not "into flag-waving" and hoped to raise their two children "without chauvinist hangups," so Walter made no sale there. And at the last house, his next-door neighbor on the other side, Mrs. Abbott apologized that she just couldn't afford it "on what Social Security pays a widow."

On his front porch Walter set the flags down to unlock the door. The box looked sadly full as he gazed at it. He pushed the door open and looked around the cul-de-sac again, lost in thought. At last he plucked his own flag from its holder, rolled it up gently, and placed it in the box.

Cassy Macrina's Book

Sometimes the arguments at the Grumpy Chef Café got pretty heated, until the grumpy chef himself, Harry Burke, or his son Terry who also weighed near 300 pounds, told people to shut up. These arguments were usually about politics or baseball but maybe not really. Ted Mitchell still blamed Johnny Grimm for messing up his knee with a cheap shot during football practice thirty years before, and some others had granddads who fought about water rights way back in the day and some women were still mad about an insult no one else remembered. Seems like some of this came out. Anyway, you'd think they'd have got pretty fierce about Cassy Macrina, too. But except for the one time they didn't and they don't, not five years ago when this happened and not now. It seems like everyone's just too puzzled to get righteous and that figures because the lawyers and the judge didn't understand it much better. Myself, I guess what she did was wrong but I don't get red-faced and shout it out. It wasn't that kind of wrong.

Maybe if Cassy were from around here they would have handled it different, just told her to stop and swept it under the rug. But she came from Cleveland though she claimed she grew up in Buffalo, New York, where her parents settled when they came from over in Europe someplace. I don't know what if any of all that is true and some people wondered if she even had a green card and what kind of damn name is "Cassy Macrina" anyway, but I do know she came here to Ritzville, Washington, about six years ago. In a town this small you notice newcomers. What I don't know and nobody knows and she never said is why in the world she wanted to move here, a place people in Spokane or Seattle think is in the middle of nowhere with nothing going for it except we have the only Carnegie Library in Adams County and the rodeo every year.

She was a pretty girl, with real black hair and eyes and a nice figure but she always looked a little sad somehow and sort of stand-offish though she did come into the Chef a few times just after she got here. I asked her out once but she said no thanks and added something funny in that strange way she had of talking: "You have something else in store, when you get smart." *Well excuuuuz me!* I thought. *Fine. Plenty of fish in the sea.* But it made me wonder if the women at the café might have a point: they said Cassy must have had her heart broken by some no-account man there in Cleveland. Probably she just didn't want to get burned again. Anyway, she got here all right for whatever reason though she didn't even have a job for six months, until she got on with the County Records.

That was a surprise. Most of those jobs go to somebody who has a connection on the County Council. Word was, when Mrs. O'Keefe retired, that Tommy Burke would get the job. He's a nephew of George Harris the head clerk. But the records were in such a mess that the County Council decided they had to get someone in there who could fix them and Cassy looked like she could fix them better than Tommy or anybody else because she had worked on some sort of records for an insurance company back east. I guess maybe she did fix things. Jim Muller told me she dug up the death certificate for his great-grandfather from back in 1920-something. Said he'd been trying to get it for months but they told him it must have got lost somehow. He was real happy to get it because he was trying to fill out his family tree and Cassy was all right as far as he was concerned.. Except death certificates are what got her in trouble.

Now George Harris is a regular at the Grumpy Chef. But then again, most everyone is including me, and sometimes my Dad, James Cornelius Murphy (I was named for my Uncle Brian but they gave me the Cornelius too, for a middle name). Well, we spend more time in the Chef since we gave up on the cattle and pigs and went whole hog, so to speak, with wheat. In winter now we don't have much to do but mend harvesters and such. According to him --George-- he noticed something funny when he went to file the death certificate for old Jack Tallman who was buried from St. Agnes church where we went, when we went, and when George went to add it to the running list they keep, a sort of register, saw that Jack's date of death was already entered. So he asked the other clerks how that happened when he just got the certificate that morning, and Cassy said she'd put it in. Now that was not long after Cassy started in Records and George said he just shrugged and figured this girl was really on top of things and must keep up with the news. But the next time it happened he saw that registry for death certificates had a bunch of new pages with death dates for a whole bunch of people who were still alive, including himself, all written in the same neat clear hand. "Date and cause of death, right there," he told us the morning after he noticed this. "Everything but the death certificate number."

He didn't want to tell us much more, though, except when he asked who did it Cassy stood right up and said she did, that it would save time later. Said they'd only have to add the certificate number that she didn't know yet. Well you can imagine. George and the other clerks just sat or stood there with their jaws dropping down until he finally asked, "How do you know when people are going to die?" She just shrugged and smiled that sad kind of smile she had.

Like I said, if it had been Tommy Burke or someone else from around here, we probably wouldn't have ever heard anything about it. But George, I guess he was still mad that his nephew didn't get the job and maybe that Cassy was making him look bad the way she fixed things he should have fixed as the head clerk, and he goes to the sheriff and says Cassy is falsifying official records and that's a crime. So the sheriff, Frank O'Keefe – he's the son of Madeleine O'Keefe who retired – he goes over to take a look and damned if he doesn't see his own mother's name there with a death date a week later. Now *he's* mad, like the girl is playing some kind of dumb joke on people. So he arrests Cassy and puts her in jail and the next day brings her to Judge Mary Muller who's a real tough judge even if she is a woman and Cassy, she says she didn't falsify anything. "Just wait," she says.

Now Judge Muller, she looked pretty ticked by something she saw in the evidence, but since there wasn't any violence or anything and Cassy didn't look like a threat to the community, I guess she figured she didn't have much choice but to let Cassy out on bail, so she did. Cassy just went home because George told her she was suspended from the Records pending an investigation by the County Council. I'm not sure George had the authority to do that but I can understand why he did, him being still ticked off about his nephew and the rest. Still, it didn't seem right.

Next morning again – this was in January so I wasn't supposed to be plowing or anything -- I was in the Grumpy Chef and this was all anyone was talking about, with some people saying the girl must be crazy and ought to get some help rather than go to jail, and others saying No, she's got some twisted sense of humor and you can't have people making up phony official records just to have a stupid joke. Actually, *that* was the one time the argument got pretty heated because people were pretty sure of what they were saying, which is possible when you don't know all the facts.

Cassy wasn't in hiding or anything. She'd walk along Main Street looking at the old Burroughs and Green houses that date way back, and go to the Safeway. Miriam Tallman, one of the cashiers there that I went with for a while in high school until I saw her talking to Jeff Hurley and got sort of jealous and then didn't give her a Valentine card so *she* got ticked off and it sort of stayed that way even if I did have a hard time keeping my eyes off her, cute as she is with that red hair and being so lively. But that doesn't matter. So Miriam says Cassy didn't buy a whole lot and nothing expensive and said – I mean Miriam said, in the Grumpy – "like she really had to watch the pennies what with losing her job and all. Poor thing." Miriam was kind of nice to people, except me.

Well, after a day or so the conversation went back to politics and baseball and the price of wheat and the weather, most of us thinking poor Cassy would probably get slapped on the wrist by Judge Muller and her real problem would be making a living because we expected the County Council *would* fire her and there aren't many jobs around here and even fewer for strangers and especially strangers who are nutty. I thought she'd just move on somewhere else. Then Mrs. O'Keefe dropped dead.

You know how people say, "Why I saw her just the other day and she looked fine"? That's what they were saying, and what a shame it was that she was looking forward to gardening and taking care of her grandkids now she was retired and here she gets carried off just like that by a heart attack no one saw coming. But they talked even more about Cassy once word got around, like it hadn't really before or we didn't really focus on it, that she had put down Mrs. O'Keefe's death date at least a week before it happened. George had let that out to somebody before they went to the judge.

Some said it was just a coincidence, a lucky guess. Others said there had to be more to it than that, but what? Harry Burke from behind the counter said, "Only way you can know just when someone'll die is if you plan to kill him. Or her." So we speculated on how and why Cassy Macrina would kill Madeleine O'Keefe and couldn't come up with anything and anyway Miriam, whose sister works in Doctor Hemmings' office, said she had it on good authority that it was just a plain old heart attack and that's that. "Besides," Mrs. Hurley said – she's Jeff's mothers -- "there's plenty of prophets in the Bible so you can't say it can't happen." I guess she knows what's in the Bible, being a Protestant like she is (Dad says her grandpa and ours used to shout "Papist!" and "heretic!" at one another), but I don't think anyone could get his head around the idea of having a prophet right here in Ritzville. I know I couldn't. But what I and everyone wanted to know was: who else did she put in that registry?

George knew, but he wasn't talking. Said the judge told him to keep quiet and everybody else who knew, like Sheriff O'Keefe. Said they could go to jail if they violated a gag rule. But I noticed that he looked at the grumpy chef a little funny and in general was quieter than he usually was. Others noticed too and when George noticed we were noticing he stopped looking around and stared into his coffee mug. Ted Mitchell asked him, "Didn't you say she put your date down? What was it?" But George said he didn't believe any of it and anyway it wasn't none of Ted's business and besides he couldn't tell him because of the gag order. His voice didn't sound as hard as his words.

One thing about living in the County Seat, you don't have to travel far to see a trial and Judge Muller's courtroom was packed when they got around to Cassy's arrangement, or whatever they call it, which I guess isn't really a trial but sort of a practice for one. Anyway, first off Judge Muller asked Cassy if she had "counsel" and Cassy said she didn't need any because she always told the truth and people laughed and I heard someone say, "You *really* need a lawyer, then!" Judge told people to shut up and said she would appoint a counsel because these were serious charges. But they went on anyway because this wasn't really a trial so she didn't need a lawyer yet. That's the only sense I could make of it. Then Jerome Mitchell the prosecutor all spiffy in a dark suit like he always wore since he came back from law school at the University of Washington, talked about a violation of article such and such and to wit this and that.

By and by the Judge asked Cassy how she pleaded to the charge of falsifying official records and she said, in this quiet little voice that you could hear real well anyway, that she was innocent because the records weren't false. Judge Muller, she looked kind of puzzled and called Jerome up there to talk in private for a minute and everyone strained to hear but I couldn't catch anything but "…demonstrably false?"

People were getting restless. No one cared about the legalities but everyone wanted to know who was on that list and hoped Jerome would read it out but he didn't. We all saw this big green book he had in front of him that had to be the registry but you couldn't read anything in it and pretty soon the judge said she was reminding all the "parties" not to divulge anything and the documents had to be sealed. I don't know if that meant they had to tear out the pages Cassy filled in or what, but we sure never saw that book. Finally she said she was setting the trial for two months later and told Cassy she'd best cooperate with the lawyer that would be provided if she couldn't afford one and we all thought, *Well duh!*, because how could Cassy afford a lawyer when she had to count her pennies in the Safeway?

People weren't very happy afterwards. Nothing had really been decided and they wondered when they'd ever get to look at those dates. A bunch of us went to the Grumpy Chef afterwards – it has beer, too – where Ted Mitchell said it would all come out at the trial. All that evidence and stuff has to be public. Says so in the Constitution. Some of us weren't so sure he knew what he was talking about just because his son was a lawyer, but we hoped he was right. Some people weren't willing to wait, and went off to Cassy's apartment to ask her directly.

Afterwards they said she wouldn't tell them anything and didn't even open the door and invite them in but just excused herself. All the same, people would go up to her on the street or in the Safeway and beg her to tell them if they were on the list or if their sick brother was going to make it or, when she wouldn't, ask her at least to suggest a lottery number or if they would ever find a husband. As all this got back to the café, it turned out she did give some answers but most didn't help much, stuff like, "you win the lottery by not playing" or "don't give up hope." But Miriam Tallman of all people got a straight answer, sort of: "Yes, you've found a husband." She – Cassy – probably made a mistake by answering like that because then she had all the single women in town asking her. I never heard of any more definite answers and that's probably why, bit by bit, people stopped bothering her and focused on the trial, where they thought it would all come out. But that never happened.

What happened instead was a couple people died. One was old Mrs. Hemmings the doctor's mother that wasn't any surprise because she was 98 years old. The day we heard about that I saw George sneak into the kitchen and talk quietly to Harry Burke, who seemed to get mad. Only thing I can figure is maybe George was telling him he ought to see a doctor because he'd seen the book and knew something. Either Harry didn't believe him or going to the doctor didn't do him any good because a week later he had a stroke and died right there in the kitchen of his Grumpy Chef café. George looked real upset after that, even though he and George had never been like best friends or anything.

Then the trial didn't happen. Instead they had some sort of hearing where Jerome Mitchell made a big fuss about "a long list of people vulnerable to emotional distress by the irresponsible actions of Ms. Macrina." Then this kid from Othello, Jerry Spring, who had been appointed to defend Cassy said there wasn't a single record that the state could prove she had falsified and the most, "the *very most*," his client could be charged with was a petty violation of the Office Regulations because she hadn't taken information directly from a death certificate. Upshot was the judge said that since Ms. Cassy had been discharged from her position (and by that time the Council really had fired her), she had already been penalized for her violation of procedure and did the prosecution really wish to proceed to trial? Jerome started a speech about a prosecutor's duty to protect people from mental as well as physical assault and the accused had put more than 500 people in jeopardy but Judge Muller cut him off asking Yes or No? He said no, the prosecution didn't insist on going to trial, though he let on like he was disappointed. Last thing the judge said was the registry had to be kept locked permanently in the courthouse, after the Records Office had copied whatever they had to copy.

No one knows quite how she did it but Cassy Macrina got out of town without anyone knowing. Must have packed up in the middle of the night. That's what we speculated a couple days later at the café, where Terry was still too depressed about his father's death to act like the Grouchy Chef, which he was now. We sort of kept our voices down, out of respect. There were times when nobody spoke at all. After one of these times Johnny Grimm said, "You know, I just can't get it out of my head that there's a book in the courthouse could tell us when we're going to die." That shut us up for another good while. In a way, maybe it still does.

Five years on, all this is starting to fade away. Folks don't talk about Cassy much anymore but a lot of us still think about that book. Cassy probably ought not to have done it because it made people gloomy, but sometimes gloomy might be a good thing. Ted Mitchell and Johnny Grimm seem like real good friends now, like that thing on the practice field never happened. The women don't make so many catty remarks as they used to. I finally gave Miriam that Valentine card and after that a ring and we got married by Father Tuan at St. Agnes where it got more crowded on Sundays and has pretty much stayed that way. Maybe Father Tuan owes one to Cassy but I don't know how he'd pay it. You can't even find her on the Internet.

Poems

A Hope for Heirs

Humidity will work its patient will
On letters boxed and stored upon a shelf;
Their fate to soften, fade, to wait until
Some heir cleans up the basement for himself.

Those boxes will be thrown in truck or car
And carried off somewhere to fill the land
And buried deep, all their accounts of far
Place and time to mix with loam and sand.

Well life goes so, and foolish to lament
That memoirs of the gone should also fade.
Yet I would hope a summer day be spent
In sharing what I had, how I was made.

The friend who left so long ago to teach
Bright and dullard students what he could
Was never -- not from China! -- out of reach
Nor I, from just as distant neighborhood.

Children born, jobs lost and got, things seen--
Iguanas, Saudi prudes, strange frogs and flies--
Spark speculation: what then does it mean
That San Gennaro's blood still liquifies?

This book or essay one had read or writ
Finds comment here, and questions, funny twist,
A play with language or a playful twit:
"How could you be so blind as to have missed?!"

It's hard to dodge that later, second, death
When last memory of your face is buried too
With one that you once knew, perhaps gave breath,
Leaving none who still can picture you.

Such the common fate when one lacks fame,
Yet I had something given but to few.
My fondest wish, that heirs should have the same:
Who you were, a friend who truly knew.

.

Advice to a Grandchild

Yes, you got here first; it seems but fair
That you should swing toward sky in almost-flight
Upon that magic chain-link leather chair,
Until you tire, or day makes way for night.

Yet Mother will insist you yield your place
To late-arriving girl half your size;
Demands you do so with some show of grace,
Suppress all pouting while another flies.

Hard lesson this, one each day proved anew,
For toddlers yet unborn will eat and grow
To seek their turn and form an eager queue
Witnessing it's time that you should go.

Their turn then to learn what none can mend;
All our too-brief flights must too soon end.

March, 2014

Springtime each November
To Giovanna, November 19, 2009

The almanacs as one agree
The equinox has passed;
Thus dark and dreary days we'll see
'Till Spring arrives at last.

I know the date, and know the sun
Must more a stranger be
Until complete his southward run,
Yet this is Spring for me.

This date was love both reaped and sown
My life began anew;
And more than summer warmth I've known
Each day I've spent with you.

Astronomers but vainly reason
When our love knows but one season.

Arlington Hotel, Dublin
July 21, 2004

Before we saw the sign, we heard
The voices, pipes, the feet --
Orgiastic drum and festive word
Reached out to claim the street.

"Arlington Hotel" writ bold
At doorside, and within
As many as the hall could hold
Swayed laughing to the din.

On tippest toe we spied the stage,
The red-haired girl Gael-clad;
Her face as somber as a sage
As 'neath her legs went mad.

Her dance from times we scarce recall,
The music ancient too,
Come current in this wood-lined hall
The earth-born joy renew.

The banjo, never native here
Joins pipes and fiddles old;
New amplified the reel rings clear,
Old tune made newly bold.

This music more than past displays
Ancestral joys and cares;
Dissolves the space between our days
Makes our hearts dance with theirs.

At the Deathbed

Strange machines in bright red numbers write
Biography's last chapter. He briefly wakes,
Looks about and sees or only stares
At the brother by his side.

They will remain unsaid, at least unheard,
The things I would have had him know.
Comfort wrung from this: he knew
What real men never say.

Yet parting's not well made
By clumsy queries in the few
And brief coherent moments.
As if years stretched ahead.

God grant he heard, when lines ran flat,
The love that I sent after.

The Best and Worst and Last of Times Retired

I imagined I'd roll over and sleep in,
A smile on my face that I need not
Stumble to the bathroom, shave my chin
And shiver in the Metro parking lot.

But not at all: I now leap up at five
Like kids on Christmas day, glad to lose
Myself in every hour, be alive
To read or write or play just as I choose.

And yet this freedom is no kind of leisure,
Imposes sterner tasks than those that pay:
Were waking hours given but to pleasure,
I know I'd fitful sleep at end of day.

From office work and meetings I am free;
The harder work, to be who I should be.

Blackberries

About as thick this year as last,
Just as the neighbor said;
But only if you dare to pass
Through brown and brittle dead.

They stretched across the public path,
Annoying honest men,
Brought on themselves The City's wrath:
Green trespass met its end.

Behind the line the City drew
Thick stalks naively grow;
Present their glistening fruit anew
As if they didn't know.

More deep than root, their yearly need
To stretch and green and bloom,
Tutor yet again their seed,
So sure the world has room.

September, 2009

Christmas Gift

"Too many gifts," we all agree, and plant
More beribboned presents on the pile,
Ashamed to be consumers, yet we can't
Embody season's joy in other style.

We're stuck in weight and measure, can't believe
Our love expressed enough, unless it's worn
Or read or played with, and conceive
That joy augments with bright red wrappings torn.

I plead tradition: that chicken was excess
That lent the peasant table rare bouquet;
And mothers' homemade dolls cost them no less
Than midnight sewing after weary day.

We know love is not weighed nor worship wrapped
Yet neither did God's gift remain in thought,
But came to us in flesh and bone entrapped,
The gift by which our gift of life was bought.

The first of Christmas gift showed us the way;
Extravagance, thy name is Christmas Day.

Different Gardens

I'd like to think this garden toil
Puts me in the way
Of Irish kin who tilled the soil
To keep gaunt death at bay

But I dare not. We hope to eat
Tomatoes by and by.
And if they fail in summer heat
Our Safeway will supply.

No Safeway then, nor pence nor crown
To buy the spuds denied.
What prayers went up as shovel down
That God again provide?

Mine a soft and different way;
They dug to live, I dig in play.

March, 2013

Falling Home

(In the Cemetery at Cloneen, near Banteer
Identified as the "Burial Place of the O'Callaghans")

A lovely thing, the earth, attracting
Blackwater from the heights to the blue sea,
As once she charmed mute glaciers into acting
As sculptors in the Valley of the Lee.

How she draws all things to her! This graveyard wall
Built stone on stone by hands grown strong and coarse
Has yielded through centuries to her call,
And stone by stone goes homeward to its source.

Those hands shaped like my own went well before
To mix with other bones in this deep loam,
Perhaps with those that once the traveler bore
Who brought my name to new and distant home.

We'll meet, we hope, in Heaven; by and by;
Please God, it harbors earth as well as sky.

August, 2004

Gianna's Travels

In mother's arms two thousand miles and more
She's flown to us in scarcely half a day
Where she has been for months in our hearts' core,
After countless years upon her way.

Her soft breath and supple legs, they say,
Gift of mutant crawling onto land
Eons ago, from out some sheltered bay,
Learning first to breathe and then to stand.

Blue eyes much like those with which she looks
At giddy *Nonna* and this strange new room,
Once studied German forests, Irish brooks,
Searched hungrily for sign of berry's bloom.

The graceful hand now reaching for a top
Is patterned after those that gathered grain
And learned at length to plant and reap the crop
That fed a village on a pagan plain.

Empires and migrations, plague and war
Scholars, skeptics, saints and famine year,
Ancestors whose names we know no more
Combined in wondrous maze to place her here.

She's learning now to crawl, and soon will know
A world of words for *mother, number, Rome.*
May she be wise, let words make marvel grow
At her own coming hence, and going home.

Grace Beyond Counting

The fingered beads are small but very clear,
Announcing clear as Gabriel the last
Hail Mary of first decade, and the near
Glory Be, Our Father, as we pass

To Second Joyful Mystery, where the son
Elizabeth and Zachary long prayed
Womb-bound leaps for joy at what's begun,
Innocent yet knowing God has made

A Covenant anew and soon to show
Within a stable, marked by star's arrest
And lowly shepherds' marvel, first to know
Eternity in time, now come to bless

And more than bless, redeem, our fallen race,
To enter in and share our mortal state,
Endure the worst, hard death in shameful place,
Our guilt too great to pay at lower rate.

All this the small beads speak as fingers slide
From one to one to one while voice intones
The words the angel spoke to Joseph's bride,
Our words imploring we not die alone.

Time told bead by bead and five times ten
May seem sometime to halt, and we know now
An instant where the Virgin is not then
But here with us, with shepherd, sheep, and cow.

Now and always now is paid the cost;
This morning's sin cuts Christ like lash or knife.
Today the angel's greeting and the cross;
Here the Resurrection and the Life.

Gray on Green

Gray on green was all that world
Beyond the fog-wet pane;
Firs and pines and Cyprus trees
Drooping in the rain.

Something waited 'midst that gray,
Something works there still,
Turning sodden trunk and leaf
To hope, and bone-deep chill.

Trees will bloom by us unseen;
A date will come to pay for green.

April, 2012

Harvest Time

*And do thou, O Prince of the heavenly host, by the power of
God, thrust down to hell Satan and all the evil spirits who roam
through the world seeking the ruin of souls.*
--Invocation to St. Michael

A wandering course led to the park,
He roamed this path and that,
Past maples and oaks sleeping, stark,
And leaf piles sodden flat.

He seemed not to see, less to savor the beauty,
The gift of brown-red, the crushed gold;
His cold eyes scanned restless, held firm to his duty,
The Nothing he'd chosen of old.

He turned at the ringing of children's bright glee,
Small mortals at play on a slide,
Sneered at such joy neither knowing nor free,
Bereft of his dearly-bought pride.

Their mothers, watchful, by low fence
He studied, not for long;
Infected by near innocence
And love, they'd prove too strong.

Down winding path he found at length
The sort of soul he sought;
A man who nursed with half his strength
Resentment in his heart.

Well begun is work half done;
He tracked the promised rage;
As darkling eve eclipsed the sun
A new blot graced his page.

In the Cemetery at Capannori

Here angels and Madonnas grow,
Heaven visions come to earth
To wait with those who lie below
The sure and certain second birth.

Few graves but have fresh flowers by,
Familiar dead still family pride.
Smooth Carrara slabs defy
Forgetfulness when tears have dried.

Yet tombs, like we, are in Time's sway,
Hard marble, too, to ruin wed;
Cracked slabs removed, they'll take away
These bones, make room for fresher dead.

We pray their names will still be known,
And ours, when God joins all His own.

October 6, 2010

Liberal Education

He demanded we not be the creatures
Of fathers or mothers or preachers;
Reading from approved shelves
We judged for ourselves,
'Till our thinking was very like teacher's.

Many Problems *Can* Make Up a Doubt

I've read and understand: the sun that sets
Doesn't set at all; it's we who turn;
But sunset beauty is, by these same texts,
A fantasy. Some things I cannot learn.

Bones crumbling in museums demonstrate
The hand with which I write was once a claw;
Nonetheless I'm puzzled that blind fate
Should kindly graft a thumb onto a paw.

We have, they say, a billion tiny things
That let us see, or make the bleeding end,
Start joyful tears when Christmas choir sings,
Yet none of them the gift of any friend.

In science only reason! That seems fair;
Yet hard to reason there's no reason there.

November, 2008

Mallow Castle

And did they serve, at end of day?
Walls thick as fear? The watchman's tower?
Guard De Rupes' usurped sway,
Hold new-planted Norman power?

Those massive walls did not stop time,
Nor Irish song that seeped through stone,
Charmed Normans with strange native rhyme,
Made them Irish, blood and bone.

Nor did they stop the Tudor god
From ravaging Sir John's bright halls,
Nor see him laid in native sod
'Till quartered corpse had graced Cork's walls.

From hand to hand they passed again
As Cavalier and Roundhead bled
Asserting Scripture's rule of men,
Avenging Charles' royal head.

Become a prize, and not a force,
The castle heart could not hold fast;
Surrendered then to Nature's course
Crumbled to become the past.

Now tourists come and gaze, and smile,
And puzzle out what must have been
Upon a time, this ruined pile
And how it served a race of men
Long gone with all that mattered then.

Is vanity the lesson taught?
That strongest castles must decay
With all things else that men have wrought?
That we are creatures of a day?
These stones have more than that to say:

Yes, we must all decay at last
But first can fashion future's past.

In 1185 the first castle was built in Mallow. In 1285 King Edward appointed Thomas de Rupe Sheriff of County Cork. The ruined castle described here "was built around 1598, either by Sir Thomas Norris (or Norreys), or his daughter who married into the Jephson family. During the Confederate War, the Jephsons sided with Parliament. The castle withstood an attack by Lord Mountgarret in 1642, but was captured by Lord Castlehaven in 1645. The castle was burnt down by the Jacobites in 1689 and fell into ruin." (from "http://www.castlestories.net/Ireland/County-Cork/Mallow-Castle.html). Giovanna and John and I saw it in 2004.

Meditation at Rush Hour

Bumper stickers all too quickly read,
I bootless stretch my neck to look ahead
To see if there's a reason for delay
Beyond the surplus cars I see each day.

Of course I can see nothing, must resign
Myself to study of this Ford's behind;
A local plate, no tourist SUV --
No comfort there: it's still delaying me.

I wish I had a small nuke of the kind
Would vaporize all cars except for mine.
The road then lying open far as sight,
This drive would be a motorist's delight!

The happy vision lasts, alas, just 'till
I drive into the Safeway where I'd fill
The tank, get doughnuts, beer, and more,
To find all dark the station and the store.

As Mother Mary said, just let it be:
Commuters in those cars commute for thee.

Naples Byw

They hide their last i
Sudden left and ri
In stairway to a smaller
Down twisting to another
To surprise anew the gilded ample square

A darker shadow starts the narrow road
A busy clever Greek made most direct
To olive groves since pressed by Roman walls
Or castle keep renewed by France and Spain
Turning in the quadrille on the bay.

He walks here still: faces in the bar
And bakery, crashing past on scooters
Repeat the oldest murals, frescoed saints'
Amaze. *Madonna col bambino*
Asked blessing at her every corner shrine.

Laundry-filled canyons, fragrant lanes,
Wend and wind through galaxies of worlds
Quick glimpsed before the nimble schoolgirl
Shuts the gnarled door on the court within
And private time, with all its teeming life.

These roads still lead to Rome, if you would go
But that is use, not purpose. A tortured circularity,
From home to font and market, altar, home,
Has turned these stones to glass; children skip
From one to next, joining ghosts in play.

Our Friend the Mole

'Neath lawn laid smooth and richly green
Disorder's agent digs unseen;
And morning shows a hill or hole
Proclaiming that here came a mole.

We have put there, and there, a trap;
There they stay and never snap.
In tunnels put the poison pills--
Seeds to grow yet other hills.

Men rise each day to put in order
Bridges, laws, and garden border;
Our labors moonrise moles reverse--
As if enforcing Adam's curse.

Surely they are Chaos' nurse.
Unless there's something even worse
Than lawns again to Nature wrought;
That deeper order be forgot.

The Weekend Crow

On Fridays Dad was somewhat late,
Pickup silent by the gate
Ten minutes nearer end of day.
The liquor store was on his way.

Two Old Crows in their place,
He disappeared to wash his face;
Grime of plumbing left behind
His smile proclaimed that God was kind.

Sunday evening saw the last
Dark Bourbon poured into a glass;
Its effect, like all before,
Not rage or rant, contented snore.

Weekdays as dry as a Bedouin's tent,
And just as dry, the long days of Lent;
How could there be any problem in this?
The money? Well hell, it'd always been missed.

A working man needs some relief
He paid for his own, was never a thief,
Missed no work, crashed no car
Beat no wife, trashed no bar
Took us camping, kept us well-fed
Fixed the roof or the sink or the bed
Caused no neighbor a bother
Honored mother and father.
And yet.

Something invited each week that Old Crow;
Our fathers have reasons we've no right to know.

On a Rainy Redwood Night

They're worth the drive, those giants
Soaring to blue sky on trunks grown all past huge,
Dwarfing not just my small frame but me,
A May-fly to the length of life in them.

A fitful night brought dark equality.
The clever camper I'd been asked to share
Has bath and stove, a marvel of design
But closed around me as the rain beat down.

Quietly, lest better sleepers wake,
I slipped out with umbrella and a light
To walk a trail and breathe the wet sweet air,
And have a talk in darkness, man to tree.

What was it like, before strange men arrived?
Before infernal engines slew your like?
Or, when did you first hear amazing news
Of revolution? Bunker Hill and Waterloo?

This was, perhaps, in your 500th year?
Well after through those southward-branching roots
You heard of caravels arrived from Spain,
Of empires gone, of new ones in their place.

To these and more, the tree made no reply,
Not even when I asked if in this grove
Lived one so old he might recall the star
That shined that distant night on Bethlehem.

It may have been a language thing,
This failure to communicate.
I'll never judge a tree.
Nonetheless, I slept the night away,
Dreaming that the Redwoods envy me.

On Finding an Old Latin Book

Il Terzo Anno di Latino. (Published in PAWA March 2010)

It looked as timeless as its subject
Indifferent to the basement clutter;
Transparent Italian title:
Third Year Latin.

Amazed and pleased she thumbed it through,
Saw margin notes she'd scrawled
These fifty years and more ago
In an other world.

Italian explanations overwhelm
Each Latin phrase, Great Caesar
Rendered silent as his *predicato*'s
Parsed at length.

"No way to teach a language," she avers;
And from long teaching this she knows.
Yet this imperfect text speaks loud,
Awakens deep-held visions

Of a hurried small thin girl
Along a narrow road more used
By horse and cart than cars,
Running late to class.

Of a classroom where a dour nun
Drones at like-dressed girls
Shivering on their stone-cold bench
Despite the night-fired brick beneath.

Of that girl mumbling by the fire
Complimenti di agento,
Hoping she can master them
Before her home-tasks call.

Of the priest whose solemn Latin
Echoes, sometimes, something
Professor Rubrichi wrote
Of *genitivo.*

Of Grandfather and Grandmother
Aunts, uncles, neighbors,
Friends and rivals, stolen play
In hard years leisure-thin.

Of a time when *America*
Was a report of distant dreams.
Of the time that made her,
Nurtured *Eram* into *sum.*

Resisting the Fall in Pisa

It still leans, the tower tall
Though maybe not so much;
Clever engineers have such
Means as thwart the fall.

New bright with centuries' grime
Now scrubbed away at last,
One fondly hopes that marble mass
Impervious to time.

Confident I'll never see
Simone's work laid low,
I'm haunted yet by fate I know
That towers share with me.

Not gravity alone
Pulls highest things to earth;
We are drawn before our birth
To collapse of mind and bone.

Men and marble, art and beasts and all
Have their seasons; the last of them is fall.

April 2012

What Saint Francis Saw

Last coffee drunk I rinse and drain
The mug. She waits no more.
Jumps up and barks and turns again,
Looks lustful at the door.

She doesn't strain the leash until
We pass the first fir tree;
At trail's head she knows full well
Old custom sets her free.

Then she to her world, I to mine,
Her nose explores the sod;
My world is random thoughts that wind
From bills unpaid to God.

She smells, I guess, a dog who made
His mark there on the grass;
Studies every bush and blade
Where rat or rabbit passed.

How high will this month's gas bill be?
Why don't my stocks keep pace?
The pattern on that maple tree
Suggests a martyr's face.

In brambles now she seeks the source
Of some scent foul and strong;
I wonder where the law draws force
Absent right and wrong.

I see no discontent in her,
No question, no regret;
No guilt or sadness to endure
No fear of mortal debt.

It's hard to picture, if it's true,
A life still everlasting;
Did St. Francis see a clue,
A present without asking?

The Garden's Not in Eden Anymore

We sighed when rain washed in a drooping May,
Wondered if our own or fathers' sin
Had set the course of nature all astray
And if reform would make the Spring begin.

Tomato plants were merely bored by June
As spite of solstice, March time lingered on;
The cloud-dimmed sun as well had been the moon
For all the gloom that it dispersed at dawn.

July but briefly coaxed the flower forth,
Too slowly August taught it green and round;
Unless the sun unwontedly stayed north
We saw no bounty from our garden ground.

Scorching sun now mocks our summer prayer
And desperately we water 'gainst the wilt
Of scorching heat in hope our pious care
May yet forestall the arid fruit of guilt.

Such years we've seen before end in reprieve,
September plants worth reaping, if not all.
Some to celebrate and some to grieve;
We reap the yearly lessons of the fall.

Termination for Cause

Sir:
I had thought the terms of our agreement
Were quite clear.
You were to provide me length of days,
Model children by a docile wife, support for same;
Keep far away all disaster man-made
Or act of your own,
And a death if not quite painless
And least sudden, without humiliation.
I in turn would confess You Creator
Of all things seen and unseen, offering customary
Praise and adoration.

Regarding line four above
Your performance has been marginal at best,
And I have now confirmation
From two physicians
Of what I must deem willful disregard
As to length of days and dying.

I therefore recognize no further obligation whatsoever
To provide the aforesaid praise, etc.,
Or, indeed, to acknowledge Your existence.

Any further communication should be directed
To my counsel,
Who assures me that he knows You
From of old.

A Different Samaritan

Running late I almost tripped
Over his sprawling grief;
Apology he offered none,
Only moaned about a thief

Or thieves: his weak and whining words
Sputtered through blood bubble,
Complained of pain and fear and loss
As if these were my trouble.

I stepped away, he grabbed my cloak
Blubbered for some aid;
All right, I gave it, sound advice:
"You see how errors are paid.

"You walked alone, on dangerous road
Despite more prudent voices;
Here you have the consequence
Of your own unwise choices."

I went my way, looked back just once,
A merchant from my town
Knelt beside the hapless wretch,
Spread over him his gown!

There was written, small but fine
The problem with such giving:
Cleaning up another's mess
Enables careless living.

May 17, 2011

To Giovanna
November 19, 2006

Forty years are fewer than before.
They stretch no more to vague infinity;
Only last week seem distant days of yore
But yesterday you said "I do" for me.

Thus if we may decades crush to days,
And live again two lifetimes in an hour,
We fear no racing sun or moon's delays:
Both 'then' and 'now' are subject to our power.

For if we can't escape the moon and sun
Which rise to count away our nights and days,
They cannot touch love always new begun
To which we wake each 'morn with new amaze.

Past and present, future we allow
But not within a love that's always now.

To Thomas on His Baptism
From Nonno

It must seem very strange, that thrice-felt breath,
Priestly hand, and salt upon your tongue;
You cannot know that they put death to death,
Begin anew your young life just begun.

You do know this: soft arms that bear you in
Are not your mother's own, though gentle too;
Godparents are a special kind of kin
Asking faith and life, they speak for you.

They declare belief, you reap the grace
Of Savior's wounds by you nor thought nor seen.
May name-saint keep you ever from that place
Where his own sterile doubt and pride convened.

Oil and candle and water end the rite,
Perfect your innocence, our child of light.

May 27, 2012

Two Men in Church

I cannot argue with him, wouldn't try
To question anything that he has claimed;
Who am I to doubt, much less deny
The merits for which he is justly famed?

No suggestion in our town he ever stole
Or cheated on his taxes, or his wife;
I've seen, myself, how full he fills the bowl
Of roadside beggars eking out a life.

Yet this publican who reeks of dark saloon
Where every sin from gluttony to pride
Is welcomed with each whore and drunk buffoon,
Admitting all, goes home more justified!

That Galilean keeps a different score
Than counting up our sins from week to week,
As if he'd have us hold it matters more
Not what you didn't do but whom you seek.

November, 2011

Proverbial Wisdom of the O'Callaghans

Better at supper by the fire than hungry in the snow.

The cook with an empty larder sets a poor table.

A wise man will not ride a dead horse to market.

A fried chicken lays few eggs).

Your married man buys no hearing aid.

It's a rare man who walks home from his own funeral

The world's unfair, and that's a consolation..

Your crippled, blind, and homeless beggar has problems of his own.

A man must spend the night someplace.

Were men not hypocrites, they'd show virtue at all.

Every widow had a husband once.

Many's the grave has a woman in it.

Arrange your paint in place before it dries.

A woman's eloquence is in her eyes, and her voice never so lovely as when silent.

Essays

In Defense of Rote Religion

Enthusiasts of the "Spirit of Vatican II" defend tacky liturgies and declining vocations with the claim that, "At least we've gotten away from rote religion." Liberation! No more going to Mass out of habit, or because the *Baltimore Catechism* told us to. But the liberation was a fraud, for which we have paid a heavy price.

The happy talk of the past fifty years tells us what to believe, just as did pre-Vatican II sermons. The difference is that it also tells us how to feel and insists we pretend we thought it up ourselves as liberated adult Catholics. Old Irish pastors never dreamed of such tyranny. If the enthusiasts really cared about "God's people" they would join me in encouraging the return of the older "rote Catholicism" in at least three senses: catechism, or rote learning; religious observance, or rote piety; and ethical formation, or rote morality. Doing so would promote more intellectual honesty, more religious experience, and more charity toward and among those Catholics who still go to church.

I - Rote Learning

In the December 1992 issue of *Crisis*, Michael Novak laments that the Church has become an "empty cistern, lacking water" for our young ("Abandoned in a Toxic Culture," p. 15). I attribute the drought to the abandonment of the rote learning associated with the *Baltimore Catechism.* That venerable series is scorned for teaching children to respond like parrots, for its lack of intellectual engagement, its superficiality and triumphalism. These accusations are largely true, and irrelevant.

The purpose of *The Catechism* was not to produce theologians or saints; it pretended to be neither the *Summa* nor *The Way of the Cross,* but to provide basic teaching about the faith. Teaching is usually inseparable from values (cf. sex education), and religious teaching can convey an almost tactile

150

sense of reality, of God, and of oneself in relation to it all. It ca[n] fill the cisterns. If we can't bring back the 'fifties we could adopt a similarly straightforward and optimistic approach in religious education.[1]

A moderately bright Catholic child could once answer such questions as: Why did God make us? How many kinds of grace are there? What is man? How many sacraments are there? And whence has the priest the power to forgive sins? Generations of such children gave rise to the old saw that "at least Catholics know what they believe." Beyond the particular doctrines, they believed in the Church and a meaningful universe and their own place in it. The *Catechism* could not answer a Bertrand Russell or Albert Camus, or quiet the doubts raised by *The Brothers Karmamazov* but children don't read these authors. Those with a philosophic bent would take their childhood faith to a Catholic university and deepen it with Aquinas or Maritain, and at coffee houses. Some lost their faith anyway, but at least they had a faith to lose.

Most children never went on to higher study and had to confront secular American culture armed only with childish learning. Yet this majority remains largely faithful, testifying to the efficacy of the old *Catechism*, and/or to a will to believe stronger than argument or ridicule. Those generations were given something solid to believe and, contrasting their stolid faithfulness with the fashionable uncertainty among young adults today even at Catholic universities, we should have cherished rather than ridiculed their experience.

In the 'sixties "engagement" and "personal commitment" became all the rage. Out with memorization and in with thinking. I mean, *really thinking* about what Jesus means to you and what you're doing for the poor of the world. And if they did not want really and truly to make their First Communion or receive Confirmation but were in class only because their parents insisted, then they should not receive these sacraments. The faith is only for the deeply committed. This was a terrible burden to place on eight-year olds or teenagers, and it was deeply deceitful.

---

[1] The new *Catechism of the Catholic Church* is very good, though not suitable for young children.

⌐

ə level, nothing changed: instead of parroting
ɪ to know, love and serve him in this world and be
ɲim in the next," children parroted "Jesus is my
"I want people everywhere to have peace and
ɲɑ⸗ᵣ. They were still not theologians or saints. But to
please their teachers they had now to pretend to some sort of
intellectual or emotional experience that they knew was
fraudulent, while their failure to feel the requisite Spirit worked
against the confidence and joy that might have been inspired by
a benign universe.

The deceit was compounded when teachers, unwilling to
reject 80% of an indifferent Confirmation class, "let on" (like
Huck and Tom in *Huckleberry Finn*) that the gangly sullen boy
staring out the window was in fact passionately seeing the
Beatific Vision or had even achieved it. At best the kids knew
they were playing a game; at worst they believed what they
were implicitly told: they had experienced all that Christianity
had to offer; small wonder they didn't and don't "get much out
of religion." The program that was to demand more (*real*
commitment) asked much less (nothing to memorize). And what
were children to conclude when they failed to have that "Come
to Jesus" moment to confirm that they *really* loved Christ? That
they *didn't* really love Him? Or that He didn't really love them?
Or that He just didn't exist? In the 'fifties we understood that
we had barely begun to climb God's holy mountain. Deep
spiritual experience would come in God's good time, if ever. In
the meantime, God expected only that we do our best.

Here I should confess my own disastrous experience as a
CCD teacher in the late 'sixties. The parish asked for
volunteers. I was given the new catechism that consisted of
pamphlets or flyers, and a bunch of junior-high students. In a
few weeks I changed their boredom with CCD into intense
hatred of myself and the Roman Church. It was easy: taking the
new method seriously, I asked them to write a statement of why
and how racism offended God. They scribbled a few lines about
Jesus loves everybody and, seeing the irritation I could not hide,
grew sullen beyond reaching. I should have let on. But how
much happier they and I would have been with an assignment to
memorize the questions and answers on the Fifth
Commandment! This they could do, and they would have

learned that God forbids anger, hatred, and revenge. Heaven help them and me; I wonder if they've been in church since.

Rote learning in the sense of passive absorption is with us always, but what do we want to learn in this way? Young couch potatoes absorb liberal dogma on "a woman's right to choose" and the rest of the political /moral agenda. So the alternatives are not rote learning and "intellectual engagement;" the choice is between "active" rote learning (memorization is work) with a Catholic purpose, and passive rote learning from the secular culture. Or rather, the choice is between learning both Catholic faith *and* the culture, or learning the culture alone, its toxicity unchallenged.

In the article mentioned above Novak cites the valedictorian at a Catholic college who "announced . . . that the primary lesson he had learned in four years was that everyone's values are relative and therefore we shouldn't be judgmental or certain about anything." For this he needed four years? Dimwitted adolescents learn it at the movies, or listening to Madonna, and it seemed the only thing my own son "got" from his Confirmation classes. I presume that Novak's valedictorian did not study the *Baltimore Catechism* in grade school. Had he done so he might still have abandoned "judgment" as a result of watching television or even thinking it through himself. But at least he would know he had broken with the Catholic Church; knowing more about the faith might have given him pause.

I doubt this valedictorian understands that Catholics should indeed be certain about the Creed, but never judgmental about persons. Maybe he still goes to Mass, blissfully unaware of the contradiction. If he does, I wonder why. It can't be for the liturgy.

II Rote Piety

In the 'sixties we learned to ridicule those "who just went to Mass out of habit," or because their parents had done so, as if it were shameful that someone should so have incorporated the Mass into his life that it became automatic and part of his heritage. So what's the alternative? That each Sunday one awake to an existential dilemma about The Meaning of It All and decide anew to take the Sacrament? To expect such agonizing is silly, though on another level people make that choice every Sunday, habitually, and no less authentically for the habit. But now they are punished for it.

With the old *Saint Joseph's Missal* one participated in the Mass by prayerfully following the English translation while the priest recited the Latin. Or not even that: simply by attending quietly while the miracle took place you did something about your relationship with God. Today "participation" means singing, shaking hands and enduring the performances of lectors or dancers or guitar players. And you damn well better feel uplifted by it all! But what if you're not uplifted by the dumb songs and artificial smiles and forced joking? What if you're only annoyed? Just as the demands on second-graders really to commit themselves to First Communion places an unrealistic burden on children, so the insistence that a middle-aged plumber or bureaucrat feel the Spirit can only leave many of us feeling resentful or inadequate or guilty. If the point is to shame us into doing better, it's not working.

How do you achieve "real participation," or know when you've succeeded? Squeeze your eyes shut tight? Hold your breath? Hear a voice or see a vision? Levitate? Whatever, the new attitude excludes the vast majority of Catholics who live and die without seeing visions or hearing voices. I readily grant something I can't confirm, that it is much more enriching to pray passionately and be shaken by the terrible hand of God than to attend Mass quietly with distractions in your head. But just as religious instruction cannot be restricted to theologians, so religious practice can't be exclusive to saints and mystics. Of course liturgists know this and, it seems to me, pretense again replaces reality as some fraction of the congregation "lets on" about "spirit" and "fellowship" that don't exist. The best is the enemy of the good and a comforting rote piety is sacrificed for an ersatz Pentecost. The old Church understood the limits of dull-witted and distracted cradle Catholics as we trooped into church, and provided us a rote-piety which constituted a real, if pedestrian, religious life. It might even have made us behave more decently.

III Rote Morality

"Thou shalt not" invites no dialogue; incorporated deeply enough, it powerfully limits choice. "Taboo" is commonly used to ridicule moral prohibitions thoughtlessly accepted, but who does not wish that Serbian soldiers had thoughtlessly accepted Orthodox prohibitions against murder and rape and torture? Or that IRA terrorists would obey priests, or that priests universally respected taboos against pederasty? Particular cases may involve pathologies immune to morality, but among the sane majority taboos regularly restrain impulse.

I once heard a parish CCD director describe a new program of "moral growth" that would encourage "moral maturity" in children and adolescents, moving them in stages from simple obedience to an ultimate harmony of will and intellect with the Creator. The goal was to produce adults making free moral decisions aligned with the Sermon on the Mount. I imagined a teenage couple parked in a car by the lake. If "Thou shalt not" fought a losing battle against the hormones bouncing around inside the Chevy like electrons in a reactor, what chance had, "You have to decide what's right for you"? This places a nearly impossible burden on youngsters, expecting them in such moments to develop or even remember snatches of philosophy about personal integrity or prudence or moral maturity. Some would do so; some always do anything. But the rates of teenage pregnancy suggest that "Thou shalt not," reiterated by Church and family, worked better. And not just for teenagers.

How many Catholic men and women grew old in reasonably happy marriages because divorce was simply too shameful to contemplate, the prospective pain on a parent's face too terrible, God's disappointment too certain? Let a mathematical sociologist can work it out. I hazard that the number was much greater than the number of unhappy couples trapped in hopeless marriages, as some surely were. Even the happiest marriages may know moments of mutual detestation, but when divorce is not an option, people mutter and feel sorry for themselves, kick the screen door and then start to forget the petty argument or to put the serious problem in perspective and eventually laugh at themselves or forgive and understand anew that they are inextricably bound to this man, this woman, and make the best of it. When the taboo is left behind, divorce may become the first option, with attendant misery for themselves and their children.

Examples could be multiplied: don't steal, don't cheat, don't join in cruelty against Jews or blacks or immigrants or anyone (the "gay-bashing" by some Catholic high school students in Washington, D.C. a few years ago shamed us all); don't lie, don't hit a woman, don't miss Mass. When prohibitions truly function as *taboos*, warning us that eternal powers condemn selfishness or cruelty, they make it much harder to justify indulgence in appetite or anger. (By way of contrast they are *not* health or beauty aids like "Just say No to drugs," the designer plea of a culture that provides no reason for denying yourself anything, not even death.)

Are such taboos effective? They must do something or they would not earn such frantic condemnation from relativists. If it's impossible to know how many men did not beat their wives because of childhood dogmas, the current moral void seems to be doing much worse. Assailed by lust, anger, greed, fear, pride or sloth, we need something equally unyielding deep in the bone to counter them: we need taboos. Give temptation a hearing and reason regularly panders will; the CCD promise of a more demanding and mature morality plays out as flabby permissiveness which validates any moral decision because it's the one I made and therefore the right one for me. Every person his/her own catechism, revised daily, and pretense reigns again: "sincerity" is attributed to any moral choice, with the further pretense that sincerity renders such decisions morally heroic. How noble to follow your conscience!

It was never a question of catechetical answers alone, nor was the choice between staying forever with rote learning and thinking for yourself. We first learn mathematics and history by rote and later analyze the logic. Some people think very little, most only sometimes, and a few very deeply. The point is to give youngsters a religion to think about. We'll always lose some kids but we can at least offer them something solid enough to reject: Joyce's Young Artist knew exactly what he didn't like about the Church, but those who fall away today may well feel they're leaving nothing unique: they can get the same touchy-feely self-congratulation on talk shows or at support groups. Psychobabble will not long satisfy such lapsed Catholics but neither will they remember an authoritative Church calling them home.

Home, one hears, is the place where they have to take you in. They just have to. Thou shalt not turn away family. It is, or was, a lesson drummed in early by word and example, made so basic a part of your psychic furniture that it wanted neither explanation nor defense. Maybe that's why we didn't hear so much about the homeless in the bad old days. The same kind of rote learning once made the God-filled universe home for all of us and, *mutates mutandis*, could do so again. Let's say a rosary that it may be so.

Homiletic & Pastoral Review, February 1995, rev. February 2015

The Rabbi on my Mind

The polemics over Pius XII and the Jews seemed to be dying down when Mel Gibson's *The Passion of the Christ* provoked renewed denunciations of Catholic anti-Semitism as well as theological questions about Christian understanding of the relation of our religion to Judaism. I think the accusations against Pius were unfair, as were many objections to Gibson. But our belief in Christ as the Jewish Messiah remains the fundamental divide between ourselves and our "elder brothers in the faith." At the same time, our long persecution of those brothers remains a dark heritage with which we must come to terms. Progress on both of these issues requires the dialogue assiduously promoted by John Paul II, and I remain grateful for the continuing memory of a moment of such dialogue. It inspired memories, and reactions, which inform a lifetime of reflections.

In 1964 Rabbi Arthur Jakobowitz visited my theology class at Seattle University, and it's hard to untangle what he said from what I thought he meant or what subsequent rumination has imputed to him. But I remember him: mid-thirties, robust with a thick black beard and a thick Brooklyn accent, a skullcap, black-rimmed glasses and a very sharp wit. I understand this describes entire neighborhoods in New York but he was unique among us and I still see him vividly after the faces of most teachers have faded away together with whatever they taught. Some of these were also witty and bearded but none spoke personally of the God of Israel or answered the Christian-Jewish question with devastating finality. And more: the meeting threw anti-Semitism into a painful immediacy that awoke shame and sorrow and fear. These burned the day into memory, as did the question he didn't answer.

The Jesuits of SU thought we would better understand the Old Testament if we heard from one who did not regard it as "old" at all, but as a continuing covenant. The Rabbi's reputation preceded him and we anticipated his appearance in "Th102" (required for all Catholic students) both because he was reputed "funny" and because for us, products of parochial schools in the 'fifties, a rabbi at Seattle U. was almost exotic, even in the third year of Vatican II. Instruction began before words, when the Rabbi and Father Patterson entered laughing like old friends. Then the Jesuit introduced him warmly. It seems very mundane now, after the Pope has visited synagogues and mosques, but in 1964 it was novel and moving.

Of course the lecture was very basic: Rabbi Jakobowitz explained that a rabbi is a teacher, not a priest, and mentioned that whereas Catholic priests are forbidden to marry, rabbis are obliged or at least expected to do so. There was some joking about who got the worse deal. His description of the Halakah shamed our ignorance while his quick history of Conservative, Reformed, and Reconstructionist movements made his Orthodox stance clear enough that we recognized a kindred soul: if he were Christian, he'd be Catholic. Then he invited questions on anything except why Jews don't accept Christ: he would deliver his set piece on that near the end. Hands went up:

Why do Jews continue to observe dietary laws when the sanitary conditions that may have inspired them no longer apply? "Because," he said, "God told us to." Maybe the laws against pork protected the Hebrews from trichinosis, but who knows? God didn't talk about refrigeration. He said don't eat pork, so we don't. And similarly with all the dietary laws: "we observe them because God said so." But, he continued, one of the effects of observing the Law in all its parts is that every waking moment of the day reminds the Jew of who he is until his entire life is lived, ideally, in the awareness of the God of Israel.

I don't know what kind of explanation I'd been expecting, but this answer seemed at once persuasive and familiar: we didn't eat fish on Friday because God, via the Church, commanded this small abstinence to remind us of who we were. The Rabbi showed our own practice back to us more clearly and as a logic we shared with him and, on a moment's reflection, other religions. Yet it was no simple "fundamentalism," but the validation of simple fundamentals by a tradition that never ceased to reflect and explore.

"Why must a rabbi marry?" asked a girl behind me. "Maybe you're not cut out to be married." To which he answered, "Maybe I'm cut out to eat pork?" There are reasons in Jewish social custom that urge marriage, but it is sufficient that

God wills it so. It was like hearing a voice from the Covenant, from one who held to an agreement with God that predated and overwhelmed any argument about its terms.

Others asked why Jews don't seek converts like other religions, and Rabbi Jakobowitz spoke about God's compact specifically with Abraham and his descendants; not for him to question God's will in this. Yes, someone noted, but there are converts to Judaism -- Sammy Davis Jr. for example. What if we all wanted to convert to Judaism? "In that case," he said, "I wouldn't be invited to Seattle University anymore." And so most of the hour passed with pertinent or dumb questions, wise and/or witty answers.

At length he turned to the inevitable question: "Why don't the Jews accept Christ as the Messiah?" I found his answer troubling because I could imagine no answer to it. Jews don't accept Christ, he said, because it is inconceivable to a Jewish mind that the Christ of the Gospels could be the Jewish Messiah. A "Son of God" is more than inconsistent with Jewish understanding of the Bible; it is contradictory and even blasphemous. So there is no point in arguing correspondences from Isaias and Matthew to decide whether Jesus was the foretold Emmanuel because on the evidence of the Christian Testament itself, this was impossible. To recognize Christ would be to disown the soul of Judaism that was to produce the Messiah.

(Israel Zolli, the Chief Rabbi of Rome, converted to Catholicism in 1945. I wonder how he countered this understanding of the Jewish soul.)

The Rabbi added some nice comments on the ethical teaching of Christianity as if to soften this blunt rejection and spare our feelings. But it was his genius that despite his having revealed a theological division more fundamental and irreconcilable than we had ever imagined, there were no hurt feelings to mend. As I then (or later) understood him, no offense could be taken; this was no denigration of Christianity but rather the faithfulness of a Jew to the heritage he had received. If it was painful and troubling to understand how utterly he dismissed the basis of our religion, it was impossible to expect him to do anything else. To understand that the Jews reject Christ in faithfulness to God presents a painful dilemma, but a real dilemma as opposed to those based on ignorance and prejudice, and the Rabbi implicitly suggested a way to deal with it: love God as you know Him; don't demand His reasons.

Today, I suppose, students would respond with an easy shrug: O.K., sure. Whatever. But in those days and in such a place the idea of religious truth still had currency. If the corresponding danger was bigotry, we had also the possibility of learning true tolerance or at least something closer to it than the current indifference which is closer to contempt. But that's another matter.

So this answer has stayed with me, and so has the question which was not apparently answered: "The Biblical suffering of the Jews is presented as part of a meaningful pattern of sin, punishment, forgiveness and restoration; do you see any meaning in the even more terrible suffering of the last two thousand years?" His tone was somewhere between sarcasm and sadness: "We just want it to stop."

It is a truism that the best teachers provoke rather than give answers and in doing so accept the risk that students may come to the wrong conclusions. So I don't know if this good man would even recognize the answers his visit helped inspire, if only by giving Jewish experience a face and a voice and an urgency. In any case, over the following weeks and months I decided that the Rabbi's seeming evasion of the question was instead the only possible response. Dostoevsky wrote that no divine scheme could justify the suffering of one little child, not one Anne Frank. So what possible "meaningful pattern" in the slaughter of six million? Better not to seek lest you create a Moloch.

But how could the Rabbi love so totally the God who had permitted this or was unable to stop it? Because, I concluded, Jewish love of God is not conditioned on understanding reasons but on something prior, on the response of the heart to God's ancient choice of his People. And the Rabbi emphasized another thing: Jewish awareness of the utter difference between God the Creator and man the creature. You don't judge God, do not bring Him to the bar of human reason or contract law or philosophy or measure Him even by our best instincts of compassion and decency. The gulf between God and man is that great.

Five thousand years of Jewish history and thought cannot be compressed into one academic hour of 50 minutes, yet I can't shake the conviction that I learned something about the 'way of being' to which Jews aspire. This surely was Fr. Patterson's motive in arranging the encounter -- this, rather than simply to meet a Jew and see that he was a nice guy. (You need no rabbi for that.). I remain grateful to Seattle University for this chance to meet a Jew precisely and purposefully as a Jew, and seeing not just that he is a nice guy but wholly and joyfully a descendant of Abraham; it proved to be one of those experiences which condition both future thought and childhood memory.

In Seattle's Madrona district in the '50's two Jewish kids usually joined the softball games at the corner of 33rd and Pine. (Center field was 'out' since that was Mrs. Nelson's front yard and she got mad when we retrieved the ball from her flower beds.) Melvin was a heavy hitter and argued a lot about close calls but he was all right. I didn't like his skinny sister much (always whining), and hardly knew his two older brothers who had gone away to rabbinical school. But there was always the sense of difference because Melvin wore that little hat like a bishop's or the Pope's and on Saturday they would ask us to turn on the lights or set the thermostat, and because they drove away each day to Hebrew School rather than attend the public and parochial schools in the neighborhood. Arguments over foul balls might end up with Melvin and his sister speaking to each other in Hebrew and laughing at us and we had no response. I mean, the small Latin of the Catholic kids couldn't compete; "Dominus Vobiscum" isn't much of an insult. So the tiresome old epithets were exchanged and we really didn't think much about them though I felt mildly guilty because my father would say gruffly "Don't make fun of the Jews" whenever the subject came up. I didn't suspect then that he had any reasons for saying this beyond good manners, did not connect it with the old black and white 8mm newsreel we watched sometimes together with the latest home movie of a camping trip. It was titled *Victory in Europe* and had soldiers diving into ditches and airplanes strafing and then the swastika on top of some arch in Berlin getting blown up and finally toward the end incredible images of General Eisenhower walking past stacks and stacks of emaciated bodies. I must have known that those were the Jews Hitler had slaughtered but they were too foreign in every sense for me to identify them with the kids on the corner.

Nor did I connect those images with the mysterious and therefore sinister old man in the dark house on Pine Street. The childish trick of ringing a doorbell and running away was doubly thrilling at that house, whose occupants were seldom seen but known to speak with a strange thick accent; from hiding we'd watch the bespectacled bald man come out and look around in bewilderment and anger. But one time I was returning from the store when others pulled this trick and the old man came out just as I passed his steps. He looked at me plaintively and asked in what sounded almost like a sob, "Can't we be friends?"

I suppose I should have made connections but I wonder why they weren't made for us or at least made more forcefully. The nuns used to say something about the Jews being unjustly persecuted, usually in connection with Matthew's Good Friday verse, "His blood be upon us, and upon our children." They emphasized that subsequent generations could not be blamed for deicide and this seemed so obvious that I wondered why they mentioned it. Sister Margaret could have told us why, could have been more informative about the Church's part in unjust persecution and warned us that phrases like "cheap Jew" are more than bad manners, are the seeds of potential horror or like an AIDS virus that over the years destroys our ability to resist hatred and cruelty and madness. Since then the Church, especially in the person of John Paul II, has done much to confront its past, an exercise as necessary as it is painful. Perhaps the pain explains the reluctance, fifty years ago, of those nuns to give us details.

Certainly they discouraged anti-Semitism. But they should have told us what anti-Semitism had produced. Did they think the Holocaust too horrible to describe to children? All the more reason to warn that the road to Auschwitz begins with childish name-calling and careless stories about how the Jewish furniture dealer cheated Mrs. Nelson. All the more reason to study and repent the expulsion of the Jews from Spain, their suffering in the Inquisition, the cruelty and injustice and the lies told for centuries, for Father Coughlin repeating them even as they came to fruition in Europe.

Had I been born in Munich in 1920, and heard official encouragement of anti-Semitism all my life, what would I have done when Melvin and his sister came to ask shelter from the Gestapo? I'd like to think that I'd have hid them, like the good gentile in Anne Frank's diary. I'd like to think that, but have no reason to believe I would not have been with the Gestapo at their door. Thank God I was never put to the test.

All this seems obvious now and you shouldn't need a rabbi to find it but in my case Rabbi Jakobowitz was the catalyst who made me revisit my 'Jewish experiences' and see Melvin or the old man on Pine street with new eyes, understand why the former asked us to set the thermostat and imagine the pain we inflicted on the latter who must have wondered if he were ever to escape the hatred. The Rabbi in my mind provided a voice as I read Shylock's "If you tickle us, do we not laugh?" and denied the caricatures in *The Merchant of Venice* or *The Jew of Malta*, and made relevant Church history the more painful. He still returns whenever I think of Jews or Judaism and I wonder if he'd recognize himself at all in my description or what he'd think of the effect he's had. I imagine him asking, "And what if the Rabbi had been, not friendly and dedicated, but dour and arrogant? Would you still feel so guilty about Christian anti-Semitism?" A fearful question: against logic and fairness we still see groups in the images of the few individuals we meet. I'd like to think the effect might finally have been the same because however obnoxious he might have been, I could yet have seen a Jew who resembled many Catholics. He would not have been an abstraction in his vices but just another unpleasant individual. Or I might have wondered why he was so bitter toward us and found some reasons. This is what I'd like to think, but I give myself too much credit. All the more reason to thank the Rabbi of memory for what he taught and what he was.

Confessions of a 'Fifties Altar Boy

There was a clear and eternal order to it at St. Theresa's: you served the eight o'clock Mass one Sunday, then the nine o'clock the next and then the ten and finished with the High mass at eleven which was a pain, lasting an hour, but the good thing was that the guys who served at eleven had the eight o'clock all week and could get to school late and even skip the whole morning if there was a funeral. For those you also got to ride in a Cadillac or a Buick to Calvary Cemetery way out past the University of Washington and if you stood by the hearse afterwards looking really sad some relative would quietly hand you a tip. So when our eleven o'clock came around every six weeks or so Mike Hurley and I would show up in the crowded little vestry at 10:45 with a sort of upbeat resignation. The guys from the ten o'clock would give us a hard time as we squirmed into our cassocks and surplices, sarcastically hoping we'd enjoy the sermon, and we'd shoot back that we hoped they enjoyed Math and Catechism on Monday while we were making five bucks apiece at Mrs. Maloney's funeral. Greg Malinkis was the only one of us who went to the seminary, and then just for a year, but we all had a nose for clerical privilege.

Mike Hurley and I were partners right from the start and for more than two years made a pretty good team, alternating "bell" and "book" amicably and not squabbling over who got to ring the bell at the Elevation. Not like some teams. And poor Quentin McPherson, no one ever saw him ring the bell: Pudgy Schwartz bullied him into accepting "book" as a permanent designation. We figured it was the name. How could a Quentin stand up to Pudgy, especially when he was giving away twenty pounds?

But like I said, the eleven o'clock was a nuisance: long enough anyway with all the sitting and ceremony it also had a sermon so you were trapped until noon, your Sunday cut in half. And then you could never predict the mood of the pastor, Father Quinn, who was about one hundred years old and redfaced and when he was grouchy he yelled at you in the vestry and whispered angrily when you screwed up during Mass or were too slow for him but sometimes the only problems was that he didn't see you standing there with the wine and water already because he was nearly blind even with his Coke-bottle glasses. Mike thought he was worse when he was drunk but I couldn't see any difference or even be sure if he was drunk. But for all that we sort of liked him, maybe because we identified with his clumsiness which matched our own. And sometimes he'd turn jovial and kid around in his rough way, asking if St. Theresa's was to be the only school in CYO that wouldn't win a baseball game all year, or complaining that if he couldn't improve our Latin the Bishop would ship him off to the Indian reservations. It was sort of a double joke because we knew, and he knew we knew, that his Latin wasn't much better than our's. Which even made us feel kind of sorry for him because at least he tried whereas none of us altar boys (except Quentin and Greg) would willingly pronounce Et introibo ad altare Dei as anything but "Ed introyboy ad altar day" lest we be thought fairies or something. Quinn seldom seemed to mind or even to notice. Not like the Curate.

In the nearly forty years since serving my last Mass I've never met anyone who inspired the awe of Father Ball. It wasn't physical fear though that was a part of it -- and strangely too, since he was never known to hit anybody. It was more, as though all the authority and wrath of God, which were just sort of understood to be represented by Father Quinn and other priests, had taken flesh in this robust young black-haired and dark-eyed Irishman. Like an Old Testament Christ. The accent had something to do with it: sometimes you could hardly understand him ("We're nan of us woorty to recieave ta' sacraments of Hoooly Mither Chaaarrch and do so oonly t'rough ta' infinite merrrcy of Christ") but we felt (at least I did) that this was the way God really talked, even if He used Latin in church. And he had God's omniscience as well. You knew by the way he looked at you that he knew what you were thinking so you'd try to think something good but that wouldn't work either since he'd know what you were really thinking even if you didn't. "Dahn't you be day-dreaming about the baseball during Holy Mass," he might say as we lined up to enter the sanctuary, as if he were looking at the image in my head of myself lining a shot right down the line, leaving Immaculate's third baseman floundering helplessly. Or he'd come into our eighth grade class and wonder if there were any boys here who had entertained impure thoughts; as if he didn't know, as if he needed our eloquently guilty faces to confirm it.

He didn't joke around much with us, at least not on a level we could understand. Sometimes we weren't even sure we were supposed to laugh, as when he said that St. Brendan taught there was a special place in Hell for boys who murdered their Latin. We got a lot closer to "Et in-troh-EE-bo ad alt-AH-ray day-ee" with him. But he was predictable so we preferred him to Father Quinn; besides, when he did give a sermon it was short and started with something funny and might give you some new way to think about the Good Samaritan or whatever. And, given the authority he projected (or which we projected onto him), whatever he said was certainly true and very important. Father Quinn usually talked about the boiler and how we'd damn well have to be cold if the people didn't come up with $145.75 to pay Nelson's Plumbing for the last time they fixed it. This was also true and important but it wasn't the same.

Father Ball did most of the weddings and there was a rotation for those too, and we were all greedy for them. The tips were better than for funerals and you could get some cake afterwards in the parish hall. Father inevitably read about husbands cleaving to wives and talked about the obligation to bring children into the world and raise them for the Kingdom of God, exhortations which got Hurley and me grinning surreptitiously at each other. We were figuring some things out even then, even in 1955, and "obligation" seemed a strange word for it. We would have said "license" if we'd had the vocabulary. Anyway, we understood that matrimony was sort of

167

a refuge from sin and we knew quite a bit about sin. The really essential stuff, anyway.

To serve Mass in those days was to take a role in an awesome drama, a divine comedy passing through despair in the Confiteor (so many grievous faults!) to reach the happy ending of expiation, forgiveness, and restored order. Of course we didn't say that, but the solemn ritual repeated time and again exactly the same forever and ever (we thought) made it clear even to the dumbest of us that this is the way things were in the universe, and the universe took note of what we were doing. Almighty God was strangely vulnerable: I could hurt His feelings just by making fun of Quentin McPherson (to mention only this). God would love me either way but He'd much prefer I ask for His help to avoid those sins which would send me to Hell. Sex, whatever it involved exactly, could be either a sin or part of a sacrament. It's up to you. With God's help, of course -- and that of the altar boys.

Looking back, I think our pubescent souls were endangered far more by Pride than by Lust, maybe because the fascination of the latter blinded us to any of the other deadlies. Well, Anger maybe: you could get in trouble for that if you really punched a guy. And maybe the nuns had a point about Sloth though neglected homework didn't seem very momentous. Avarice and Gluttony were for old men and we were too smart to commit the stupid sin of Envy which (Father Ball said) brought no pleasure. No, it was Lust that increasingly fascinated us, how to avoid it or get away with it or even know what it was, and all the while we were apprentice Pharisees with one foot in the sulpherous pit.

We knew that a priest could say some sort of Mass without an altar boy: Father Ball did so most days at six a.m. in the Convent. But a Mass in church without altar boys was unheard of. So they needed us to have a Mass, and you needed the Mass to have the Eucharist, which you needed if you were to get enough Sacramental Grace to overcome the temptations of Anger and Lust and (for all those old guys out there) Avarice and Gluttony and so on. If altar boys were all to die or go on strike or something the whole damned parish would go to Hell. No wonder the Knights of the Altar was the classiest organization in school, with pins and meetings and officers; it was special and exclusive even if almost all the boys did get into it by eighth grade. Girls didn't, of course, but it never occurred to us to think less of them for that reason (until recently, there had been little reason to think of them at all). Nor did we think we think we had a monopoly on the Faith; the girls were a lot better in Catechism than we were and surely more saintlike. Some of them. We thought. But altar boys were really important cogs in the machinery of salvation, just like the pardoners before us.

If we were special within the parish, we thought ourselves much more so in relation to the public school kids, heirs of that pathetic historical disaster the so-called Protestant "Reformation." (It was only after I'd flunked into a public high school that I saw the word Reformation without quotation marks.) Not that we didn't have Protestant and Jewish friends, some of them closer to us than most classmates; but we talked to them, or played catch, across a gulf. Not a gulf of "misunderstanding" and still less of hostility though the occasional fight might include some sectarian epithet ("Dumb Protestant!" "How about the Inquisition?" etc.) But they were "them," a nation outside the embrace of Mother Church. Both the nuns' teaching and our own impulses led us to regard these kids with more concern than antagonism and we comforted ourselves that a nice guy like Jerry Pierce surely had Baptism of Desire. Maybe once or twice I even prayed that God would convert or at least help the poor bastard, cut of as he was even from Sanctifying grace except maybe a bit from Baptism of Desire and how far could that carry him?

The larger world was similarly categorized and clear: the University of Washington housed Protestants and worse, atheists and agnostics who lay awake nights thinking on evil they might to to Mother Church. Whatever that place might produce of value, like the football teams with Hugh McElhenny and maybe some engineers or doctors or even good Catholic lawyers like Al Rossellini (later Governor), we knew they wallowed in the most absurd error and ignorance. The Jesuits at Seattle University could confound them all left-handed. So could Sister Margaret and the other nuns; so, for that matter, could we. "By faith" answered whatever the Baltimore

Catechism didn't. And we'd learned from Sister Ann how post-"Reformation" European and American history were largely the chronicle of futile heretical attacks on the True Church against which the Gates of Hell could never prevail anyway. Protestant folly would have been funny if it wasn't so sad, with millions of souls lost and Catholic martyrs dying for the Faith. Like Saint Thomas More. That's why they had the Constitution protect freedom of religion in America, and Catholics signed the Declaration of Independence. It's good to know all these things by age twelve or thirteen, even if you learn pomposity too: pride gets knocked down soon enough but the benign certainties remain to warm a lifetime.

Later, the certainties would be attacked more fiercely at Seattle University than at the University of Washington. The Jesuits were into "challenging blind faith" whereas the 'sixties radicals at the UW had come around to respecting any, like, faith system as long as you didn't try to, you know, impose it on others. But a Knight of the Altar could fearlessly send his mind out to joust with Jesuits or radicals since all the while his heart stayed snug in God's keep. A bit cowardly, perhaps, but why not? St. Theresa's had given us an ordered Cosmos and to exchange it for the intellectual anguish of fashion seemed a poor bargain. Besides, you could get credit for intellectual honesty without making the trade. I mean, it really doesn't cost you any important certainty to acknowledge that John XII was perhaps not even the worst of many rotten popes, that Jews have good Jewish theological reasons for not accepting Christ and good historical reasons for detesting the Church; or that Luther condemned real abuses and that theology is not mathematics. Or to realize that one believes finally because he wants to believe. "It's a free choice, not determined by history or personal revelations or pure reason." You could sound fashionable after all in the mid-'sixties, when everyone was reading Sartre and Camus.

It was also in the 'sixties that Father Quinn died in some rest home for priests, and that Father Ball returned to Ireland. So I heard much later, long after I had moved from St. Theresa's and even from Washington State and old classmates were harder to find on every return as we were spun off to California or Montana or South America by the same fates which had brought our parents to Seattle in the first place. The old neighborhood went through the classic urban cycle to gentrification so I couldn't afford to go home again even if you could go home again and even if the fates permitted. But if it were possible, I'd surely take my children.

Such altar boys and girls as I see these days seem to have no clear duties in liturgies laboriously created anew each week with progressively worse and longer results. Father Tom and Father Bob are painfully well-meaning and sincere but their unavoidable preaching, like that of Sister Ellen, isn't very precise. I think they're saying that God will love me no matter what I do so long as I stay open to the Spirit and don't invest in South Africa. There's a lot about the Spirit and the People of God. My children, alas, don't respond well and that's probably my fault but I just wish they could have seen a Mass where the ancient forms imposed awe and dignity and no liturgical coordinator invited us to dance, and that they'd heard about a God who cared enough to get mad. If Father Quinn's dogmatic certainties inspired us to smugness or Pride, Father Bob's reluctance to define or condemn anything invites Despair. I was never tempted to invest in South Africa, and if there are no serious rules about sex or your Sunday obligation then maybe there's no serious Rule-Giver either and what I do doesn't matter because I don't matter. But the kids' first reaction is boredom: who needs this mush anyway? You might love or despise Father Quinn and his dogmas but it's hard to feel anything at all about gentle Father Tom who talks only about feelings; you just want to get away.

It should be clear by now that the crowning sin of a 'fifties altar boy is to become a tiresome conservative in the 'nineties when Father Greeley has polls showing most people don't want the Latin Mass nor real Irish priests neither. So I stifle my complaints and silently thank Sister Ann and Sister Margaret and Fathers Quinn and Ball and others now in the Communion of Saints for having taught me the important thing that's happening there on the altar behind the yellow balloons and the children's paintings. But sometimes you want to talk to someone else who remembers the Cosmos so on my next trip to Seattle I'm going to look up Mike Hurley and we'll agree that they don't make them like Father Ball anymore and what would

Quinn say to that Curran guy or to these radical nuns and hasn't everything gone to hell since Vatican II? There will be a great shaking of heads. Besides, Mike married early and might have grandchildren serving Mass now and we could teach them something, if only how to get a tip without seeming to ask.

Catholic Universities, a Lament

*I may give away all that I have, to feed the poor
. . . if I lack charity, it goes for nothing.* - St. Paul - "

In one of the many requests for money that I have received from my alma mater, a university "in the Jesuit tradition," I read that 75% of the school's students do volunteer work in the community and at a rate more than twice the national average. One can only applaud. But applause will not drown out dissatisfaction with a university that seems aligned not with the Catholic Church but with her enemies. Charity is not the only theological virtue. Faith and Hope also make demands.

Helping the poor is a Catholic obligation but not a Catholic monopoly: Jews donate generously, alms-giving is one of the five pillars of Islam, and Protestant churches help people around the world. Bill Gates gives away his money, corporations support many causes, and fraternity members at a local state university volunteer 70,000 hours annually. Americans increase their charitable giving each year, especially after disasters, and food banks are everywhere. So the battle for "giving back" goes well. Other battles go very badly.

Catholicism has long been an "Other" in America. Protestants thought Catholics disloyal citizens because they had a prior loyalty to Rome. Of course they had and should have this prior loyalty, just as Protestants regard the Bible as the word of the Creator who gave us inalienable rights long before Congress existed. Though the "Know Nothings" who burned convents are long gone, and anti-Catholic bigotry apparently disappeared with the election of John Kennedy, the conflict endures. Some don't want to recognize it, and some fight on the other side

Abortion and "gay marriage" are symptoms of the conflict, but not its essence. The deeper issue is ontological: what is the nature of being? Catholics and others believe God is the source of being and truth. Secularists believe the universe has neither creator nor purpose and that truth is for us to determine. Though political debate seldom or never uses these terms, they are nonetheless in play. Is marriage something real, instituted by God, or a contractual arrangement created by legislatures? Are *good* and *evil* only adjectives or also nouns?

No one can impose belief about these matters, nor should one try. Christian evangelization seeks to persuade, inviting people to Christ. (Insofar as forced conversions took place, they offended both victims and doctrine.) But the Church can and must witness the faith from which moral teaching follows. A Catholic university has no reason to exist if it doesn't practice this deeper charity.

While a university is not a parish or a seminary, faith should inform all it does. Aquinas has no place in a chemistry class, but his theology assures us chemistry is possible, that rational and hence discoverable laws govern molecules. Faith insists upon the value of all people, including those of other beliefs, and I remember gratefully the visiting rabbi who spoke to my theology class about Judaism. I also remember the implicit lesson: respect for others didn't compromise what the university itself professed.

Whatever the intentions of Father Jenkins, and however faculty and students at Notre Dame understood the honor paid to President Obama in 2009, they professed the belief that abortion is not so very important, whatever the local bishop thinks. Any disagreement with the President paled to nothing as the University honored a man who (like the similarly-honored Governor Cuomo) opposes any effort to protect life. If Notre Dame lauds such politicians, why can't Catholics vote for them? Too bad about the dead babies, but we need hope and change. Did they "dialogue" about Church teaching that a unique human life begins at conception? Or simply grant the Pope, and maybe God, the right to their own opinions?

Popular culture endorses the politically correct notion that opinion is all there is: "whatever works for you." The Church insists that truth exists and matters enough to die for. You cannot be on both sides. Whatever orthodoxy the university I attended may teach now in class about faith and morals, public witness endorses neither. The university website boasted that a professor from the law school supported "marriage equality" in the California courts. "The Vagina

Monologues" are presented on campus without any attempt to counter its dehumanizing themes.

Why take Church teaching seriously when a prominent "pro-choice" politician is added to the faculty, or when two professors publish a "Catholic" defense of abortion? In 2008 a newspaper reported that 100% of faculty political contributions went to Barak Obama. It's a peculiar "diversity" celebrated in alumni appeals: people of different colors and orientations all thinking alike.

"Social justice" is one of the things they agree on, claiming the Catholic mantle as they do so. As if "social justice" was all Christ really cared about. Who needs the Pope when you have the Sermon on the Mount? True enough, the Vatican also advocates social justice, though I'm frustrated by the lack of specificity from various popes. They insist the poor must be a priority, but don't say what that means in terms of policies though they vaguely warn against a too-intrusive state. The vagueness invites us to fill in the blanks.

Unless I've missed something, university social activists regard the state as the unique means to justice (taxes and social programs). When they also leave the definition of life and marriage and education and every other important issue to the government via elections or laws or judicial decrees, they are very close to Mussolini's "All within the state, nothing outside the state, nothing against the state." Fascism was all about social justice, and it can work both ways.

Pressure to conform is always great, in ancient Rome or 1930s Italy or 21st Century America. Some clergy also conform, so we ought not be surprised that so many of our universities refuse to be "counter-cultural." Still, I'm disappointed. In implicitly endorsing "cafeteria Catholicism," a university denies fidelity to the Church. If our schools believe that the Pope is the successor of Peter, empowered to teach definitively on faith and morals, they don't persuade their graduates. At Georgetown University a poll found that "60% agreed strongly or somewhat that abortion should be legal" and "57% said the experience of attending a Catholic college or university had no effect on their participation in Mass and the sacrament of reconciliation."

Maybe I just don't understand the deep faith of these schools and it's none of my business anyway. But I know what hits me in the face, and it *is* my business where I send my money. I want my donation to support education that is Catholic. It would be wonderful if scandal never arose among a devout faculty, and if graduates could articulate the reasons for their own faith. This was never the case, though we were once closer to it. It would be nice if Catholic universities again made clear their mission to strengthen the faith of their students. If even that is too much to hope for, I'd settle for this: that students learn the principle of non-contradiction and recognize that claiming to be Catholic, while ignoring what the Church teaches, is to live a lie no matter how much soup you ladle at the homeless shelter.

They're Still Roaming

And do thou, O Prince of the heavenly host, by the power of God, thrust down to hell Satan and all the evil spirits who roam through the world seeking the ruin of souls.
--Prayers after Low Mass

A remembered cartoon from a long-ago catechism sums up the dignity and dangers of life: a devil whispers in a boy's left ear, urging him to steal an apple, while an angel on the right ear exhorts him not to do so. We got the point: it wasn't about apples so much as about our eternal worth and responsibility amid the minefield of moral choice. Heaven and Hell compete for your eternal soul, but you choose.

I don't think children see such cartoons anymore; at least, my own children did not. I can't remember the last time I heard a sermon about the devil and I don't understand the silence. If these old images were sometimes ludicrous they nonetheless taught an important truth and an urgent lesson. Soon enough we move past apples.

At about the age when temptations become more interesting, one is urged to relegate the devil and angel to the realm of outgrown toys and Santa Claus. Few people willingly admit they think possessed little girls exist anywhere except Hollywood. But if one is to remain Catholic he cannot simply discard belief in the Enemy who tormented Job, or in the demons which Christ so prominently expelled and for the expulsion of which the Church continues to train exorcists.

We learn, from Screwtape's legions, to treat the devil as a "real fiction" in the sense of "projection," i.e., real only in the sense that people truly have delusions, and to consider Christ as a sort of poet. Doing so both denies the constant teaching of the Church, and reduces our present sense of worth and dignity. Instead of *temptations* we imagine we experience biological or psychological urges growing from chemistry or from something that happened in kindergarten. Instead of having eternal souls for which Powers compete, we become organisms assailed by neurological quirks as mindless as germs. Of course the desire for worth and dignity can in turn be called a motive for projecting devils. Then again, Satan would have us so regard it. Or so I project. But the child I once was, reminded at every

Mass of those evil spirits roaming the world, thought it all real enough. Nothing in the empirical or poetic worlds has convinced me I was wrong. Indeed, the Holocaust and daily reports of sadistic murders show us evil beyond human imagining.

I've heard various crimes ascribed to "low self-esteem," suggesting that people might do evil just to prove they can do *something.* As if to inoculate children against this danger, various school systems have abolished failing grades because failure damages a student's sense of self-worth. The silliness of such projects is another issue, but there is a core of truth here: we all need to feel we are valued. So it is the more puzzling that we have discarded the traditional imagery of angels and demons competing for us, imagery that affirmed the unique eternal value of every man, woman, and child. We are prizes for which God and Satan contest, and ours the power to choose between them. We have moreover the almost unimaginable power to offend God Himself by our cruelty to a classmate or to a stranger, and the power to please Him with kindness to colleagues or to the poor of the world, or simply by praying to Him. Even our suffering has value, and the good nuns encouraged us to "offer it up." How much more "self-worth," "empowerment," or "adulthood" do you need?

I would like to see this brought back, and I know I'm not quite alone. But it won't be easy because many people, including priests, want nothing to do with anything that smacks of pre-Vatican II practice. A new literary genre (call it "Old Church Bashing") decries the "narrow pre-Vatican II mentality" and the pervasive fear of hellfire or (about as bad) the pastor's anger. Various writers bitterly recall a patriarchal hierarchy treating the faithful as sheep, and those sheep attending Latin Masses of which they understood nothing. Others claim there was virtual silence about God's love, while sex was feared and loathed, tolerated only for the production of children.

I can't argue with other peoples' memories but I recall few of these things, and never in the exaggerated terms in which they are now presented. Far more memorable are the pervasive sense that God so loved us that he sent his Son to redeem us. Further, that Christ and Mary and the angels are so intent that we should participate in that Redemption that they are with us always against the wiles of Satan.

One can anticipate the angry reaction to any attempt to recover the practices that fostered my memories: "Today the Church is *really* about love! God loves sinners unconditionally! That's all we talk about!" Well, yes. But, I ask, What sinners?

At funerals we used to pray for the eternal rest of the deceased, that all his sins would be forgiven. I would hope the poor man or woman had at least made it into Purgatory. Going straight to heaven was possible, but probably not a realistic hope. Today a funeral seems more like a canonization when the priest confidently asserts that the deceased is smiling down on us from Heaven. I heard this recently at the funeral of a man who wasn't even a practicing Christian, let alone Catholic. Trusting that a charity beyond my comprehension led to his burial from a Catholic church, I pray the deceased is indeed in Heaven. But confidently to proclaim it in this way is to trivialize both the funeral Mass and the man or woman being buried. We speak of them as if they were all their lives moral children, incapable of seriously offending God. Praying for them is pointless. Maybe that's why funerals seem less and less an occasion of prayer and more like a 50th anniversary party, decorated with photos of the honoree in youth and age, wearing his favorite fishing hat.

Still, many people remember the old days as excessively negative and simplistic. I can agree they were often simplistic, but no more so than the present when our naive ideas of Heaven and Hell have been reduced to a childish idea of Heaven alone. In all times the problem is that most people end their religious studies in childhood or adolescence, and Sunday sermons do not and perhaps cannot replace the additional reading that would make the basic simplicities more compelling. But preachers could try.

The idea of being thrown into a fiery pit is vivid enough but invites questions, quite aside from "How could a loving God do such a thing?" How can fire affect an immaterial soul? Or is the fire spiritual? Will it change when we get back our material bodies? Are those devils doing a good work as they torment us? And so on.

We can no more know what eternal torment is like than we can know what eternal happiness would be in Heaven. (Is it like being in church forever? Sitting eternally in a "Life Teen" Mass? That sounds more like Hell.) But we can know ourselves better: Dante's *Inferno* is all about the torments we choose, and eternally knowing what we have chosen to be. Carnal sinners are blown about by winds, just as they chose to be blown about by passion. Misers and Spendthrifts roll dead weights, image of the gold they worshipped. The violent boil in blood, the element they so cruelly spilled. In sum, those in Hell had willingly wed themselves to the instrument of their torment. Were the fires of Hell to go out, and all the demons and centaurs and other monsters vanish along with the blood and the weights and the winds, the damned souls would eternally remain what and where they chose to be: alienated from themselves and God. If Dante's depictions of Hell must also seem simplistic compared to the reality, preachers might nonetheless borrow from him to better engage mature intellects. And so with our images of Satan.

Horns and cloven hooves? Those are images from another time. The cold breath and guttural laugh of the devil in *The Exorcist* are perhaps more timely but in the end they too depend upon costume, makeup, and sound effects. All our attempts to picture the embodiment of evil and of nothingness must finally seem silly. But perhaps we can hear that malign nothingness in the inner promptings to anger or avarice or excess, better than we can picture it. In any case, we see its effects: violence and child molestation and fanaticism and egoism and so much more. The recent films *Hotel Rwanda* and *Downfall* depict Evil without horns or cold breath. It has a human face.

So why not ask again that St. Michael the Archangel "cast down to Hell Satan and all the evil spirits who roam through the world seeking the ruin of souls?" They are still roaming and seeking but, in their very malevolence, attest to our worth and our power. If Satan cannot be kept cast down in Hell, we can make him an unwilling catechist.

The Curmudgeon's Catechism

The publication of *Summorum Pontificum* has been a double blessing: it promises to make the Tridentine Mass more available, and has reduced family arguments. I need no longer convince relatives that I have not joined the Pius X Society or the Sedevacantistas.

Pope John Paul II's *Ecclesia Dei* was not widely understood, but many Catholics know that the new *motu proprio* has encouraged and even mandated the old liturgy that was only permitted by the earlier document. Nonetheless, I'm still asked why I drive fifty miles to a Mass I "can't understand" when there is a church just fifteen minutes away.

I grow uncomfortable. If I express a preference for the Latin Mass because, e.g., it has bells, I seem to imply a criticism of the English Mass, which typically does not. I'm not interested in criticizing the *Novus Ordo,* the ordinary liturgy of the Church and the one attended by the vast majority of Catholics now and in the future. If it's good enough for the Pope, it's good enough for me; I'm happy to attend on feast days and some Sundays when otherwise I would have no Mass at all. At the same time, the Latin Mass is also good enough for the Pope. The trick is to explain my preference for this option in such a way that relatives will think of me only as odd, and not hostile--and maybe not even that odd.

The subject doesn't lend itself to the short pointed responses of the old Baltimore Catechism. It could hardly be otherwise since the answers we memorized were just that, answers and not arguments. Their logic was the teaching authority of the Church. Since that authority has eroded over the past forty years, and because I can claim no authority anyway, I offer a sort of rhetorical catechism along the following lines.

Question 1. Why attend a Mass you don't understand?
Answer: But (a) I do understand; (b) no one understands; and (c) not understanding is the point. The question refers to Latin and the first answer is that one can understand it both by following the English translation on the opposing page of the missal, and by repetition: I know that *introibo ad altare Dei* means "I will go into the altar of God" without consulting the translation or parsing the grammar or even thinking in English.

Of course I must consult the missal to follow the Introit and Communion and other readings of the day, and doing so requires me to pay close attention to what the priest is reading at a given moment. Similar attention must be paid for many Ordinary parts of the Mass such as the Lavabo or the Invocation of the Saints. (Maybe this, along with acclamations and responses and hymns, is what *Sacrosanctum Concilium* had in mind when it called for the faithful to take a "full, conscious, and active part in liturgical celebrations.") True enough, some priests speak more clearly than others and sometimes it is hard to know just what the celebrant is doing. But you need never get far out of synch, and soon enough it becomes clear that we have now reached, say, the *Orate Fratres.* Consequently, when someone objects, "I don't understand Latin!" I gently suggest that they could indeed understand with active participation.

On another level I don't understand at all. When the priest reads from the Preface that the Father, Son, and Holy Ghost are one God, *non in uníus singularitáte persónae, sed in uníus Trinitáte substántiae,* I don't comprehend this any better by reading on the opposite page, "not in the oneness of a single Person, but in the Trinity of one substance." This is, as John Deedy notes (*The Catholic Fact Book*), one of those "revealed truth[s] beyond the power of human understanding . . . which would not be known except for God's revelation." That is, a Mystery, one accepted on faith in the *Novus Ordo* as well as the traditional Mass. And while the *Novus Ordo* has changed this part of the Mass, it presents us with the same limit, i.e., stating something we "understand" on a linguistic level, but cannot comprehend. For example, the following from the Creed: "We believe in the Holy spirit, the Lord, the giver of life, who proceeds from the Father and the Son."

If such statements sound more mysterious in Latin, this is all to the good. One of the perennial temptations is to think we know more than we do, or can. But as Job was forcefully reminded, God is beyond our comprehension. Reason can teach us some things about God, and Revelation even more. But we cannot dissect the uncreated Creator and we are not in awe of puzzles we have solved. "Understanding the liturgy" also means understanding the limits of what we know and awareness that infinity lies beyond those limits. If liturgy includes understanding the lessons of the gospel, worship means loving and adoring and thanking the Father Who is beyond all comprehension.

Question 2: Didn't Vatican II change all that?
Answer: No. The document on the liturgy said, "The use of the Latin language, except when a particular law prescribes otherwise, is to be preserved in the Latin rites." Latin was banished later. If the Vatican II document permitted wider use of the vernacular, the Council Fathers nonetheless foresaw a liturgy in which "the faithful may also be able to say or sing together in Latin those parts ...which pertain to them." As Pope Benedict has repeatedly made clear, Vatican II never intended a break with tradition.

Question 3: Aren't you trying to turn back the clock?
Answer: In a sense, but this is a foolish metaphor. On the literal level, we set back our clocks every Fall. On the metaphorical level no one seeks to return to the past, which is impossible. But we often "turn back the clock" in the sense of reinstating a previous condition. That's why we have auto insurance. Those of us who prefer the previous arrangement of the liturgy don't want to go back in time but rather to bring the tradition forward with us into the future.

Question 4: How can you expect people to go back to the days of tyrannical pastors and "pray, pay, and obey"?
Answer: Let's not confuse boorishness and rubrics. Some people have, or claim to have, memories of an oppressive, intolerant, arrogant, and distant clergy from before Vatican II, and worry that any return to the old Mass would mean a return to the Bad Old Days. This objection raises difficulties: my own memories of the 1950's are far more positive than negative, and the negative ones are mostly of the Christian Brothers and their unpleasant pedagogy. (God forgive them, surely they taught as they had learned.) But my positive memories don't disprove what others claim to remember. Noting the obvious, that there is no causal connection between liturgy and the personality of clergy, hardly touches the emotion of this objection. Asking whether there is any less tyranny practiced by today's liturgical

and music and other committees may win reluctant nods but little more, so one can only note that insofar as laymen have taken over various clerical functions, this could have happened without changing the Mass. More broadly, positive developments over the past forty years (such as the improved relations with Jews and other faiths, and a more humane pedagogy) could, and probably would, have occurred in any case. But finally, complaints about the Bad Old Days are not about the Mass at all.

Question 5: What's the matter with the new Mass?
Answer: Nothing.

Question 5-A: So why do you want to go to the old Mass?
Answer: Between two good things, we may prefer one or the other. One reason I prefer the old Mass is its familiarity, or consistency: it is always the same, even if a High Mass includes incensing the altar and other things absent from the Low Mass. Whichever it is, the familiar ritual puts me in that attitude of worship long nourished by the same forms. The Gregorian chant always sounds familiar, even as the text may change. With the new Mass, on the other hand, one doesn't know if he will have a Mass as mandated in the General Instruction of the Roman Missal, or one with variations ever new. One priest includes a general absolution, another does not; at some Masses we recite the Creed and at others we skip it. And it seems there is always new music, much of which tempts me to uncharitable muttering. Thoughtful people have found theological ambiguities in the new rite, and especially in some of the translations. Those issues are beyond me. What does concern me are the electric guitars right next to the altar and applause for birthdays; they distract me, sending my thoughts far from where they should be.

Question 6: Isn't it demeaning to receive Communion on the tongue?
Answer: No. At least, I don't share the view of a recent letter in our Archdiocesan newspaper in which the writer objects to the idea of a "distant" Jesus "who can only be received on our tongue, because our working hands are not worthy." That's

hardly the point. Indeed, I would grant that my tongue, which has uttered blasphemies and curses and insults, is even less worthy to receive Jesus than are my hands. Of course we are unworthy to receive Christ in any way, and recognizing our unworthiness makes the gift of the Eucharist the more wonderful. Yet we are forgetful creatures, and need reminding.

When we were told that the Eucharist may be handled only by the consecrated hands of the priest, and must be closely guarded against any accidental desecration, this reinforced our awareness that it was a very special, very holy, most extraordinary thing -- the Body of Christ himself. There is no logical reason that Communion-in-the-hand should diminish this awareness, but I strongly suspect that it has. My grandparents would be scandalized to see a man in Bermuda shorts handing out the Eucharist to people in tank tops. They knew that Communion deserves and demands all the respect we can bring.

Granted, the distribution of Communion by four or six Extraordinary Ministers does speed things up. At the Latin Mass, distribution may take ten or fifteen minutes as opposed to the four or five needed at an English Mass. I accept the delay, for the waiting also reminds me that I am about to receive an awesome gift.

Question 7: Isn't it better that people are empowered in the new Mass, taking an active part in the readings and distributing Communion?
Answer: See Questions 1 and 6 above, on active participation and reverence for the Eucharist. Of course any gift benefits the giver, and insofar as people give of themselves to read parts of the liturgy or take other roles, this is a good thing. If as a result of these activities they feel closer to God than they would otherwise, then yes, that is better. But there is much more to consider.

When a layman reads the Epistle the role of the priest is reduced, leading some to wonder why his role should not be reduced yet further. Why should the priest alone read the gospel? Why should he alone preach or consecrate the Host? One hears of parishes where lay men and women are gathered around the altar as if co-consecrating, and why not? Again we have an instance of attitudes getting ahead of logic: there is no necessary connection between lay readers and a diminished regard for the unique role of the priest, but in fact these practices have corresponded with a view of the priest as just another member of the community, albeit a kind of specialist. If the unique role of the priesthood is still accepted by most Catholics (and I believe this to be the case), it is nonetheless on the defensive.

Beyond that, one may ask about the effect on the congregation, the vast majority of whom do not read or distribute Communion or play in the band. If most people only sing along, are they participating as fully as those with speaking roles? Moreover, the congregation must endure many bad performances as sincere but poorly trained lectors stumble over words, or give dramatic readings which call attention to themselves rather than to the text. Nonetheless, many people say they prefer the new Mass with all these features, and I don't ask they give them up. But for myself, those lay readings are yet another reason to drive downtown.

Question 8: But isn't it good to get away from Masses that are all about the priest?
Answer: Yes, and that is another reason I prefer the old Mass. In the traditional liturgy the priest is indeed the dominant presence. But Father Murphy is not the dominant presence. The precise rubrics of the old Mass determine every word and gesture so that Father Murphy (or Martini or Muller or Mtenga) disappears into his role as celebrant. Of course he doesn't lose his personality, which will manifest itself in tone or movement or posture; but the prescribed rubrics minimize such manifestations of individuality so that the priest acts as completely as possible in the person of Christ. I am aware of which priest is celebrating, but the Latin Mass itself changes hardly at all. This is very different from the new Mass, where the liturgy often seems an expression of personality.

An example: in the Latin Mass all priests pronounce the words of Consecration in a low voice bowing over the altar, the tone and gesture of one priest virtually impossible to distinguish from those of another. In the new Mass one priest will say the words in a low even voice, another will shout them, or punctuate them with dramatic pauses and a variety of gestures. There is no mistaking Father X for Father Y, and you must remind yourself that it is, nonetheless, the same Mass. Certainly we notice the difference and I know people who will attend only the Mass of Father X when they have any choice.

Such choosing is not entirely new. My father used to get up for a 7 a.m. Mass for the sole reason that at that hour the sermon was kept under five minutes. If the poor man were alive today I suspect he'd join me at the old Mass, not for any great love of Latin but because it usually has briefer sermons.

The Latin Mass I attend takes about seventy minutes, and the sermon seldom lasts more than seven. A nearby English Mass takes perhaps fifty minutes, of which at least fifteen or twenty are preaching[1]. That is, the sermon seems the dominant feature of the new Mass. The local priest speaks well, his sermons informed and well structured, witty and engaging. People love him. So far, so good. But if one objects to liturgy being "all about the priest," he should prefer a Mass that is all about worship.

Question 9: Aren't women invisible in the old Mass?
Answer: No. I see many women in church each week. All right, that doesn't answer the real question which is, whether those asking know it or not, Why can't women be ordained? And that is not a question about the Latin Mass. Pope John Paul II did all he could to settle this question and I address myself only to those who accept Church teachings. But the question refers us back to the Mass, in which we are all "invisible" in the sense of subordinating ourselves to worship (see above on Father Murphy becoming invisible inside the celebrant). I'm content to be invisible; I don't come to Mass to be seen or to see other people, though I very much value the social hour afterwards. In another sense, we are all visible, the whole Body of Christ. I am acutely aware of my fellow Catholics in the pews beside me or

---

[1] I'm not sure why the Latin Mass now lasts longer than did the hourly Masses of my childhood, but suspect reverence explains it. The priest proceeds with great deliberation now. Back in the day, he might rush through the readings in order to finish the 8 a.m. Mass before people arrived for the nine o'clock one.

in Chile or China when reciting the Prayer for the Living, and of my ancestors in reading the Prayer for the Dead.

If some women are pained by the absence of women in the sanctuary, and altar girls, I am sorry for it. I can only urge that they focus on the purpose and reality of the Mass that exalts us all.

Question 10: But no one wants the Latin Mass, and won't it create division in the Church?

Answer: Overlooking the contradiction in these objections, the answer is No and yes and yes and no. Pope Benedict took great pains, in issuing *Summorum Pontificum,* to emphasize that we have ordinary and extraordinary celebrations of the same rite. There is no reason that those thousands attending a Latin Mass should be seen as "separated" any more than those attending a Spanish Mass, or a "Folk Mass" or a "Children's Mass." Nonetheless, the fact that people ask this question suggests a division looms or already exists.

It was the new Mass that sparked a clear division, when Archbishop Lefebvre found it, and some aspects of Vatican II, so unacceptable that he refused to celebrate the *Novus Ordo* and established the Society of St. Pius X, which he led into (a debatable) schism when he was (apparently) excommunicated. This is very painful, and it would be even more painful if Catholics faithful to the Magisterium were to view others as less than fully Catholic. I acknowledge the danger: we are all vain proud foolish beings and may be tempted to regard ourselves as having "the real Mass" while considering others as more or less benighted.

I grant further that we who attend the old Mass are more subject to this temptation than others because we are very aware of the *Novus Ordo* and cannot help making comparisons. Others have no reason ever to think of the Latin Mass. Our defense against this as against all temptations is fidelity to God and His Church. While we hope that the Pius X Society will soon reconcile with Rome, we should pray for the humility not to act as if we were more Catholic than the Vatican -- or than Vatican I, or Vatican II.

Question 11: At the Last Supper the Apostles didn't follow a translation in a missal, so why should we?

Answer: The Mass is not a theatrical representation of the Last Supper but an unbloody renewal of Christ's sacrifice. The fathers of Vatican II confirmed this even as they wanted to accent "the concepts of community and love" (Deedy). The Mass is a ritual with defined words and gestures. If we want a precise reenactment of the Last Supper, then there will be a full meal served to men (and no women) seated around a table. Nor will there be many Scripture readings or organs or guitars.

Finally, there is a question which is seldom asked but which seems always present: Won't I be forced to attend the Latin Mass I dislike? Of course not. I assure my relatives that the only Latin Mass they will ever have to attend will be the one at my funeral.

My catechism usually ends in exhaustion rather than conversion, with relatives muttering, "Well OK, you go ahead if you want to." But sometimes one of them muses that it might be nice to attend a Latin Mass for old times' sake or, if too young to have memories of it, to speculate that it would be interesting to see what it's all about, but not at the cost of driving fifty miles. This gives me yet another reason to hope that *Summorum Pontificum* will be widely implemented: were it convenient for people to attend they might discover riches they had forgot or never known and realize that they can have it all, both the contemporary Mass and that of the Ages. Pope Benedict reminds us that both of them belong to us; to reject either is foolish and ungrateful.

.

Something *Sí*, Yanqui No

How does a country define itself? The subject has inspired both scholarship and bloodshed. At a small conference on *Chilenidad* in Concepción, Chile, I heard academics and others try and fail to pin down the national identity.

What does it mean to be Chilean, beyond the tradition of *empanadas* and local music and honoring the flag? What's the essence? To be born in Chile would seem to be part of it, but citizenship includes nationality only in a legal sense. What does your Chilean passport say about you? That you are Spanish? No, though one speaks Spanish, except for perhaps some Mapuche or Aymara natives. The father of Chile is Bernardo O'Higgins, but few think themselves Irish. Catholic? Not necessarily. Of European culture? Yes, except for the Chinese, African and other immigrants, and the Aymara and other native peoples who complicate the question enormously. Participation in the *fiestas patrias* and other traditions is part of it, but patriotic holidays are rather a manifestation of identity than its essence. Positively, most agreed that a real Chilean has read Gabriela Mistral and Pablo Neruda if only in school, and knows about Arturo Prat, the Chilean Navy officer who died heroically at the Battle of Iquique in the War of the Pacific. Beyond that, they found little that characterized a Chilean as opposed to a Venezuelan or Argentine. The meeting broke up in good natured frustration: of course there is such a thing as *chilenidad!* It's . . . something!

Such discussions of national identity could take place anywhere in the Americas, including the United States. But in the US we are wonderfully distracted; characteristics be damned, we are what we do. Americans won independence and the West and two world wars and sent a man to the moon and invented jazz and rock & roll and built the Panama Canal and avenged 9/11. We've built a shining city on a hill and the whole world admires it, or should. It all seems very confident yet it cedes this: Our sense of ourselves depends in part upon the recognition of foreigners. Consider that obnoxious chant at the Olympic games, "USA! USA!"

Latin Americans also define themselves, in part, against others. Their identities began for the most part with a war against Spain and are strengthened by commemoration of heroic leaders. As George Washington has a monument in the national capital, so José Artigas is represented in Montevido, Bernardo O'Higgins in Santiago, and Mariscal Sucre is perched high atop a column in Quito. And so on. You want to know who we are? Look: we're revolutionaries bold in battle.

Brazil seems an exception to this pattern. The most impressive statue in Rio is that of Christ the Redeemer. Is this because *cariocas* are particularly aware of their sinfulness? Or because the war for Brazilian independence was relatively short and bloodless? In any case, something's different, as if the country has been redeemed. Friends who worked in Brazil regarded assignment elsewhere as exile from paradise.

So far, so good. However, revolutionary history takes you only so far because national identity needs periodic renewal. Fights against neighbors help and the Paraguay and Chaco Wars, etc., are duly remembered. But the patriotic unity they inspire soon gives way to messy factionalism in which "identity" becomes a disputed banner. Uruguayan Colorados and Blancos both claimed the mantle of Artigas. The winners in such contests can brand the losers as traitors, but those traitors, or their families and followers, are still in the neighborhood, their discordant voices complicating the national heritage.

Foreigners serve national identity better. I heard Chileans themselves joke that a visitor can barely get off the plane before hearing that Chile has two Nobel Laureates (Mistral and Neruda), as well as beautiful women and excellent wines. Who would argue? They also joked about their hunger for world recognition of these things, and their obsessive interest in the Miss Universe pageant, where Miss Chile inevitably lost. The poor girl would then be criticized for her hair or her answers or for not being a real (dark) *Chilena* rather than a tall blonde Nordic type, as most Miss Chiles were. Recalling the agony of these defeats made me wish I had been there for the thrill of victory in 1987 when Cecelia Bolocco Fonck (a brunette!) finally brought home the Miss Universe prize.

Sports inspire even more thrill and agony. Uruguayans savor their two World Cup victories. My family and I shared the national jubilation when Chile qualified for the 1982 World

Cup, and the national despair when they were eliminated. Brazil deserves to be known for more than soccer, but none can doubt the importance of it when suicides follow a loss. One may think it all mysterious or absurd but it's real: our team won, the world knows we're champions. I'm a champion. A Chilean cartoonist, Renzo Pecchenino ("Lucas"), made a wry comment on this in 1982 after Argentina had invaded the Falkland/Malvinas Islands: an Argentine soldier tells a puzzled Falklander, "Congratulations. You're world champions." And so they were, until the British reclaimed the islands. Anyway, Spain won the Cup a few months later.

Would that sports and beauty pageants sufficed, and foreign admirers supplied whatever part of identity depends upon them. But for some or many, especially young people, they don't. Enter the foreign devils. In Uruguay and elsewhere, I met students who could recite a litany of US crimes against Latin America: 1850, intervention in Nicaragua . . . 1903, Panama stolen from Colombia . . . 1911, Honduras . . . 1954, Guatemala. And so on, up to last week. Maybe the universities have courses on the subject, with reading lists that include Eduardo Galeano's *Memory of Fire* and *The Open Veins of Latin America*, and *Century of Terror in Latin America: A Chronicle of U.S. Crimes Against Humanity* by Luis Suarez. Early and late, Latin Americans are victimized by others — by Europeans of course, but especially by North Americans. How does this view of history affect their image of themselves?

Surely the great majority of Bolivian plumbers and Argentine doctors and Chilean grandmothers lose little sleep worrying about who they are or about history. They are wise. In Ireland, 800 years of struggle against the British made that struggle itself a part of Irish identity, one that still produces horrors in Ulster. Though the histories differ greatly, some Latin Americans think of themselves in a similar way.

Of leftist revolutionary rhetoric there is no shortage. The following, from a website of the National Liberation Army of Colombia and dated July 4, 2011, is in a long tradition:

> We rise inspired by Guevara and Fidel, Red and Black like the Cubans of the 26th of July Movement, the Nicas Sandinistas, the Chilean Miristas and the ELN of

Bolivia and Peru, among others. We consider ourselves part of a continental confrontation against Yankee imperialism. We are of the fighting group who believe that the Patria is America and beyond that, that Patria is humanity.

Such interweaving of the fight against imperialism and nationalism also informed the speech given by Salvador Allende in 1971 in Rangagua, on the nationalization of the copper mines. He declared it a day of "national dignity and solidarity" tying all Chileans to the past glories: "Here we feel . . . the past, the heroism of those who fought and sacrificed their lives . . . . Here . . . is the image of O'Higgins and here we can say to the father of the country that we are his legitimate heirs."

Augusto Pinochet in turn claimed that his 1973 coup had saved Chile from international communism and restored national independence and dignity in the spirit of O'Higgins. Many agreed, citing the month-long visit of Fidel Castro in 1971 as proof that Allende had taken direction from abroad. Many disagreed, claiming that any military coup denied Chile itself. But that argument wasn't so much about Chilean identity as about which betrayed it more, the chaos of the *Unidad Popular* or the oppression of dictatorship. Surely the Chileans were this: a people who deserved better leaders.

Cuenca, with its many bookstores, proclaimed itself the most literate town in Ecuador. There I saw a large banner across a university building that proclaimed, *El futuro pertenece por completo al socialismo.* Perhaps it does, but why should students in Cuenca celebrate a future belonging completely to socialism? The agricultural economy of the Andean highlands seemed rooted rather in feudalism than capitalism. I think the appeal was the promise that Cuencans too could play on the global stage, opposing the Colossus of the North. One ought not to read too much into student slogans, but he may ask why they need slogans at all. There is something in many young people that's not content with a quiet life in a literate Andean town, something that wants to do more and be more. You'd think with all those bookstores they'd have learned from Pascal that all our misfortune results from "not knowing how to sit quietly in a room." Had the *Tupamaros* and *Miristas* and *Montoneros* known how, they would have spared their countries not only their own terror but the more systematic violence of the dictatorships they summoned from the deep.

Older people assured me that while everyone has some complaint about the United States, if only our ignorance about them, all this revolutionary nonsense was a fashion of the young, most of whom would soon enough put on a tie and start selling insurance or settle down to motherhood. (*Machismo* was part of the identity.) Some remembered their revolutionary days with a fond shake of the head, as if unable to believe that they had once been so young, so confused about the important things.

An old cartoon has two American expatriates in a Paris bar. The older man says to the younger, "You punk! I was hating America before you were born!" I can't imagine two Latin Americans in that cartoon. I met none who didn't claim to love their country however much they detested the government of the moment or criticized local custom.

During my last year in Uruguay a saying became popular: *Como Uruguay, no hay.* There's no place like Uruguay. Does that mean they know who they are? Probably yes. Well enough. We're *something,* and we like it. Even though Uruguayans can resolve questions about origins no better than Chileans, they know their country is home, contains their family and *colegio* and friends, favorite team and beaches in Punta del Este, and is the land where Spanish is spoken in the familiar way. If Latin Americans no more than others can sit quietly in a room, they can go out to apply their intelligence and energy and education to building their lives and their countries. Then they party contently at *asados* with *empanadas* and red wine while shrugging off problems of the distant world. As things are, North Americans can't imitate that attitude. But we can envy it, and our envy might be received as a compliment, maybe even a kind of apology.

Proof

Made in the USA
Charleston, SC
18 April 2015